Biblical
DREAM
STUDY

Biblical DREAM STUDY

CAROL OSCHMANN

BIBLICAL DREAM STUDY

Scripture quotations marked KJV are from the Holy Bible, King James Version (Authorized Version). First published in 1611. Quoted from the KJV Classic Reference Bible, Copyright © 1983 by The Zondervan Corporation.

Scripture quotations marked NKJV are taken from the New King James Version. Copyright © 1982 by Thomas Nelson, Inc. Used by permission. All rights reserved.

Scripture quotations marked NIV are taken from the Holy Bible, New International Version®. NIV®. Copyright © 1973, 1978, 1984 by International Bible Society. Used by permission of Zondervan. All rights reserved. [Biblica]

Scripture quotations marked NRSV are taken from the New Revised Standard Version of the Bible, Copyright © 1989, by the Division of Christian Education of the National Council of the Churches of Christ in the United States of America. Used by permission. All rights reserved. Website

iUniverse books may be ordered through booksellers or by contacting:

iUniverse
1663 Liberty Drive
Bloomington, IN 47403
www.iuniverse.com
1-800-Authors (1-800-288-4677)

ISBN: 978-1-5320-6441-8 (sc)
ISBN: 978-1-5320-6442-5 (e)

Print information available on the last page.

iUniverse rev. date: 12/11/2018

The Old Testament of the Bible

covers the history of creation until the
coming of God's son, Jesus.

The New Testament of the Bible

covers Jesus' life and the beginning
of spreading the Word.

Is that the end?

Not yet written, or written in myriad places, is the story
of the Holy Spirit. God did not stop working with us at the
end of the New Testament. The Bible is not yet finished.

To understand the Holy Spirit, we need to understand
the messages in the dreams the Old and New Testament
are trying to teach us.

Dedicated

To seekers of truth
With thanks to my dream circle
And a special thanks to Katy Zatsick, a member
of my dream circle, ARCWP (Roman Catholic
Women priest) and a Carl Jung Society member for
her many insights and additions to this work.

CONTENTS

PART 2   MECHANICS

INTRODUCTION

The Bible has Dreams

Have you ever looked at the dreams in the Bible as lessons for you? Perhaps they appeared as just an interesting part of history. To me, for a long time, they were interesting children's stories taught in Sunday school.

Seldom has anyone looked for lessons in the dreams recounted in the Bible. I wondered what Joseph, Abraham, Solomon, and others, and their dreams, have to do with us? Are their dreams put in the Bible to move a story along or is there a real lesson for us in the dreams about our communication with God? The Bible's story of dreams begins with Adam's experience in the middle of the night.

The very first time we see something happening as someone sleeps (in the Bible) comes in Genesis 2:21-22, when God made Adam fall into a deep sleep, and while he was sleeping, took one of his ribs and created Eve.

We have been spending a portion of each day sleeping ever since. Could God create something wonderful from us also? I'm assuming you believe Adam having a companion was a wonderful thing. Is there something else, something we need that God could bring forward out of us in our sleep?

The good that God has meant for us often goes unnoticed. My belief is that we are often given choices and we often chose wrongly. Why? Over the years, Dad and Mom, older brother, teachers, and others we met, said we couldn't sing; or maybe making a speech in front of a group of people was hard for us; or someone told us we weren't meant to be a doctor. We've received these various false impressions over the years about ourselves from well-meaning relatives, friends and teachers. Things like which career we should pursue are told to us as young people. We've not only believed these well-meaning people (except maybe the older brother!) but a wrong way of thinking about ourselves has been planted and gained strength over the years.

Especially strong has been what religion we should believe. Left out completely, probably, is whether we should find meaning in our dreams. There are some things we need to find out for ourselves. One misunderstanding, due to our parents not knowing better, is the importance of having a spiritual experience, most often in your dreams. Many of us never have a vocation to follow or have never been excited about our future until too late in life, if at all.

If you write down your dreams each night, you'll soon come to recognize you are communicating with

God Himself. The Bible will then hold more meaning for you.

If God had something wonderful to tell us, as with Adam and Eve, we would need to delve deep into our sleeping hours, to bring it to consciousness. Our path would first be made known to us in our dreams. We don't always understand our dreams but making the effort will make the process easier. Just rereading your dreams after a few weeks can give you a feeling that someone greater than you is walking beside you.

Dreams are mentioned 134 times in the Bible according to the New Revised Standard Version Unabridged Concordance. Of those 134 times (plus one more – Adam's mid-night miracle) only two have a negative connotation, which I am able to explain away later in this book. In addition, some people feel the book of Revelations is a bunch of scary dreams about the end of the world. This adds to the list of dreams and adds to the validity of dreams, as I will explain later.

Here I list those 134 verses in case you wish to refer to them yourself. I find it necessary, however, to get a feel for what is going on in the story, to read the story surrounding each verse. I have not included the words of the concordance for the sake of simplicity and therefore some books seem out of order or repeated due to the subject word; Dream, Dreamed, Dreamer, Dreamers, Dreaming, Dreams. Also, a reference is noted twice due to the word being used twice in one verse.

BIBLE VERSES ARE TAKEN FROM THE
NRSV CONCORDANCE - UNABRIDGED

"Reference Church of Christ, taken from the
ancient Greek translation of the Hebrew Bible"

Dream - Genesis	20:3	20:6	31:10
31:11	31:24	37:5	37:6
37:9	37:9	37:10	40:5
40:5	40:9	40:9	40:16
41:7	41:11	41:12	41:15
41:15	41:17	41:22	41:32
Judges	7:13	7:13	7:15
1 Kings	3:5	3:15	
Job	20:8	31:15	
Psalms	73:20	90:5	126:1
Isaiah	29:7		
Jerimiah	23:28	29:8	
David	2:3	2:4	2:5
2:6	2:6	2:7	2:9
2:9	2:26	2:28	2:36
2:45	4:5	4:6	4:7
4:8	4:9	4:18	4:19
4:19	7:1	7:1	
Joel	2:28		
Matthew	1:20	2:12	2:13
2:19	2:22	27:19	
Act	2:17		
Additions to Esther	10:5	11:2	11:4

11:12			
2 Maccabees	15:11		
2 Esdras	10:59	11:1	12:35
13:1	13:15	13:53	
4 Maccabees	6:5		
Dreamed - Genesis	28:12	37:6	40:5
41:1	41:5	41:11	42:9
Jerimiah	23:25		
David	2:1		
2 Esdras	13:1		
Dreamer - Genesis	37:19		
Dreamers - Jerimiah	27:9		
Zechariah	10:2		
Jude	1:8		
Dreaming - Isaiah	56:19		
2 Esdras	10:36		
Dreams - Genesis	37:8	37:20	40:8
41:8	41:12	41:25	41:26
42:9			
Numbers	12:6		
Deuteronomy	13:1	13:3	13:5
1 Samuel	28:6	28:15	
Job	7:14		
Ecclesiastes	5:3	5:7	
Isaiah	29:8	29:8	
Jerimiah	23:27	23:32	29:8
Daniel	1:17	2:1	2:2
5:12			

Joel	2:28		
Zechariah	10:2		
Acts	2:17		
Wisdom of Solomon	18:17	18:19	
Ben Sira	34:1	34:2	34:3
34:5	34:7		
2 Esdras	13:19	14:8	

You may refer directly to the segment I mention and form your own opinion. As I said before, you and only you, with the help of your higher power, can do that. Visit some of the verses I've not talked about, you may find insight into something I've not thought of or experienced before.

My biggest forward steps in my spiritual, physical and mental life happened when I first started paying attention to my dreams, about mid-life. It was all gut-based instinct, trying to know myself as I had no one to tell me what was happening to me. There are other ways to interpret dreams and these I will lay out for you when we get into the stories.

Several years later, I was able to attend the Hadden Institute where they teach a four- year course in dream interpretation. You spend a couple of long weekends each year in camp, but most of the work is done at home by mail. I was able to meet almost all of the leading dream researchers at the time. Bob Hadden is an Episcopal Priest and the setting was in the Carolinas at Kanuga Episcopal Camp.

Many people I've met since I started my solitary

dream work, who discussed their dreams with me, have received new life and new opportunities, as happened to Adam. The new beginning started with a warning that they were headed down the wrong path. When we realize this truth, the dream will tell us a better way to go. We can also ask. I have often written a question for God, prayed over it before sleep and put it under my pillow to get an answer in my dreams or have it imbedded in my consciousness when I woke.

Back to the Bible. Did you ever realize how many dreams are in the Bible, and wonder why? The Bible is a teaching book. Nowhere does it say not to follow your own dreams, it says the opposite, by giving us examples like Jacob, Joseph, Mary, Daniel, a pharaoh, Solomon, convicts in jail, Moses, shepherds in the field, and many other accounts of people's dreams. I've counted 134 times the word 'dream' is mentioned in the Bible. We'll look at some of these and see what they would mean to us if we had them today. That way, we can look for direction from the words in the Bible.

The people in the Bible knew their dreams were messages from God. They knew dreams were their pathway to direct two-way communication with their creator. By recording these happenings, repeating the stories to others, they have attempted to teach us as well. And I am one little bit of proof that this still happens. In my first book, "God Speaks in Dreams" (available on Amazon) I tell of the many miracles, changes brought into my life through God and dream work.

Parts of our culture have denied learning through dreams. They hang onto one verse out of 134 and do not try to understand the story around (or the real context of) the verse. I will talk more on this later in this book. The way we think about dreams may be a matter of belief passed down to us from parents, teachers, church, our culture; all supposedly smarter than we are. Then, there can also be laziness on our part.

Let me say, if you've ever experienced one miracle, you will want to know more, to experience more. If your very livelihood depended on catching and heeding the messages in your dreams, like the people in the Bible, and the American Indian tribes in our country, we would have put more importance on catching our dreams too. The Indians could dream about a herd of buffalo heading their way when they needed the meat for an expected long, cold winter, and because of the dream, they were ready to go after them when they came. Next time you feel a herd of buffalo is headed your way, for good or bad, turn to your dreams.

I can't help but wonder what we have missed by not paying attention to our dreams. Would the disasters of our lives not have happened had we all learned to follow our dreams? There is a book titled "The Third Reich of Dreams," by Charlotte Beradt and Bruno Bettelheim, that can be bought on Amazon (although it's quite expensive) about Charlotte, a news reporter, who lived in Germany all her life up until World War II. She had a secret hobby of writing down dreams from people she met. She escaped to England and then to the USA during the war and wrote her book when she realized its relevance to Germany, leading up to the war. Her co-author says the dreams showed how Hitler controlled the populace through dreams he gave them. After reading it, I disagree. I see God warning the people of the coming events and warning the people that they must fight back, but they never did.

One dream was had by the owner of a large factory. In his dream, military men marched into his plant and demanded he convert to manufacturing weapons. It is an interesting read and just one of the remarkable books I learned about from other dream researchers at Bob Hadden's school.

There are several different kinds of dreams, such as anxiety, nightmares, answers to problems, predictive, lucid; to name a few. Reading the various dreams in the Bible, you can see the same kinds of dreams we have each night.

My belief, and I'm not alone, is that dreams are our own two-way communication connection to our creator. Ever go to sleep with a problem and wake up in the morning with the answer? How do you suppose that happened? Therefore, the phrase, "sleep on it".

We've forgotten how to go to sleep and communicate with our creator. Therefore, we often forget who we really are. Through listening solely to our loved ones, we often get a false understanding of ourselves. Well-meaning parents want to make us into the best people they can but perhaps there is a deeper, more meaningful destiny for us. Keeping a dream journal can lead you deeper into knowing who you really are.

Everybody dreams. Watch the movements of the sleeping baby or puppy or kitten. Science has proven that we all dream. In fact, science has proven we would lose our sanity if we did not. What we lose, over the years, is the ability to recall our dream. It works much like a muscle. We lose the power of this muscle if, over the years, we have ignored it or outright said, 'no more dreams.' You can bring dreams back by making them a priority in your life. Repeat constantly to yourself, 'I will remember my dreams.' Read books on the subject, talk about it to whomever you can.

Put a pad and pencil or recorder next to your bed. Write down the date, and then write 'I will remember my dreams,' and go to sleep. If no dream is remembered, write how you feel or what is going through your head as you wake. Sometimes something will happen during the next day that will make you realize, this was in your dream. Write it down. Then the next sleep time, start with the date again. Take a large drink of water. As you wake to go to the bathroom, wait and think about what was going through you head. You'll remember longer. Soon you'll be getting snippets of dreams or feelings. Write them down as soon as you can because they will disappear. After writing it, forget it, go back to sleep. In the morning, try to understand it. Some are really easy to understand, others deal more with your emotions and need interpreting.

Nightmares are a favorite subject of mine as they can bring a swift change for the better into your life. As soon as you understand the message God is sending you, the nightmare will not come again. Your life will change for the better. The same goes for recurring dreams. From little recurring dreams, big nightmares grow. Catch the message before it becomes a nightmare!

It is like following someone along a path and trying to get his or her attention. Maybe they've won a new car, or a million dollars and you need to tell them. You call their name and there is no response. You pick up a pebble and throw it at the person's back. Still no answer, frustrated, you pick up a two-by-four and hit them over the head. This is God's way, with nightmares, to get your attention. I know I'd be mighty frustrated trying to tell you something that will improve your life if you kept ignoring me. My guess is this must be how God feels with us at times.

Once you "catch" or remember the dream, then act on it. Write the dream down, draw a picture, tell someone, buy a toy or statue honoring the dream, set it on a shelf of dream symbols. If you can do something, do it. If there is a food either add it to your diet or take it away. Do you know how many promises you've made to God over the years and not kept? This honoring the dream is all about listening to God in your dreams.

As a teenager, I'd stand in church, praying with everyone but saying my own words. "God, please don't let Grandmother know I did (this or that), I promise not to do it again". Within a short time, I forgot my promise and did it again. The time to bargain with God comes to an end. We must do all we can to prove our seriousness. God is communicating with us. You can join the ranks of Jacob, Moses and the rest in making that a two-way conversation. God and his angels are waiting.

Metaphorical images such as an egg, and new green plants, or an actual happening, like words and music to a new composition, the solution to a problem, a leap in research will come to you. Writing your dreams regularly is a small price to pay for the deep truth revealed to you. It is a small price to pay to learn two-way communication with your creator. We bury ideas and opportunities because our pre-conditioning tells us we can't do something. Go to sleep with a pad and pencil next to your bed and when you wake with a dream still active in your brain, write it down. Make use of God reaching inside you to pull out the good you can do.

God reached inside Adam while he slept and brought forth a new life. What new life lies buried in you? You don't need to understand the dream, just open that dream door and see what new opportunity comes into your waking life. Often you will first need to change a few attitudes. The dreams will lead you. Persistence will pay off. Open that dream door today.

CHAPTER 1

Abram – Abraham

Genesis

Abraham had many encounters (face-to-face, in visions and in dreams) with God. It is easy to go beyond believing and <u>know</u> God exists when you experience one of these encounters. The feeling of face-to-face happens for you when your dreams give you great advice, predictions come true, or you see a loved one who has passed on.

I've even seen writing on a board (does that remind you of the saying about the writing on the wall?). The writing warned me not to continue an unnecessary relationship I was following. The other people in the group would ultimately reject me because of my belief about dreams. It was better that I left first. God has used this way of communication with us since time began. You are truly thankful when you have received advice like that and wish for more.

Abraham was best known for leading his son, Isaac,

up on the mountain where he had been told by God to sacrifice him. This may have led to his son, Isaac, not fully appreciating God and passing that belief to his first son, Esau.

Abraham totally knew God. He had many conversations with God. He relied on God's leadership. I'm not sure why he had to prove himself. After Abraham had bound his son, laid him on an altar and raised the knife above him, an angel of the Lord stopped it, directing Abraham to a ram that was in the bush behind him, to sacrifice instead.

Abraham went to a length we probably cannot conceive to prove his loyalty to God. God will not ask this of you but will ask you to change things, like perhaps an attitude necessary to bring about loving yourself. He'll show you the way.

Abraham was also known for fathering the child, Isaac, with his wife Sara when they were both 100 and living until an estimated 175 years old.

Abraham was also a key player in the story of Sodom and Gomorrah. He negotiated with God to save his nephew Lot and his family from the destruction of the two cities.

Although he and God talked easily, there is one story, Genesis 15; 12-16 where Abraham fell into a deep sleep and was told in his dream a story of 400 years into the future that his descendants would suffer, why they would suffer, and when it would end. This is not included in the concordance under the word 'dreams', but it clearly was God coming to Abraham in his sleep.

My premise is that we can learn something about

our own lives from the dreams of the Bible. They are more than a retelling of history, so I searched my heart. Were there any instances where I would want to receive news like this? We are often given tough times in life and it might be helpful for us to understand why. That could be a part of what scares people away from dream study. Still, the warning of a death of a loved one, for instance, can prepare us, save us from a trauma that could physically hurt us. Or, maybe you will be needed to be the strong one in the group.

If I was living in a war-torn country, I may be asking God daily, 'when will this end' or 'what should I be doing?' If something terrible was happening to me or my family, I'd like to know why and what I could do about it. This kind of dream has happened to me and to those people with whom I've discussed dreams. Illnesses have been cured by asking our dreams for an answer. Understanding, and therefore a decrease in stress, can really lighten a load besides getting us on the path of good nutrition or exercise.

Going back to the dream, it clearly seemed a nightmare. Nightmares are a favorite of mine to search within for an answer. Once you find the message, your life will change forever, for the better. God often must hit us over the head to get us to listen.

CHAPTER 2

Isaac and Rebecca

Abraham's son Isaac seemed protected by God, perhaps in atonement intended for what had happened at the altar. In Genesis Chapter 20:1-6, is the story of Abraham's wife Rebecca being passed off as his sister to save Isaac from a king he feared. The King of Gerar took Rebecca, as she was a beauty. That night, in the King's dreams, God came and told him to let Rebecca go. God told him the truth of the lie and why. God promised if Rebecca was returned to Isaac and no harm came to any of them, no harm would come to the Kingdom of Gerar either.

The King of Gerar was about to make a wrong decision regarding Rebecca. Receiving information about Rebecca and Isaac in his dream helped smooth out the lives of Rebecca, Isaac, and the king.

I believe the lesson in this story is that if you are about to make a wrong decision, and you are remembering your dreams, you will make a better decision. I've had this happen. In one dream, my grandmother hauled my husband and me through her double front doors and then slammed the doors. I didn't listen and went along with a business deal we never should have touched. Sorry, Gram, for not listening to you.

Sometimes someone you know will be in your dream. Be sure and share it with them as the King of Gerar did. You might even joke about it like, "stay out of my dreams…." The person may be a total non-believer. There are many lessons for us in these dreams of the Bible.

The King of Gerar, Isaac, and Rebecca all benefitted from his dream, first by not making a huge mistake, second by exchanging many friendship gifts of food, stock and land, and lastly, finding an understanding of each other. The King of Gerar made a connection with God and with Isaac and Rebecca in his dream.

When I have a person I know in my dream, I will drop them a letter or make a phone call and let them know what I dreamed. Unless I know this person well, I often pass the dream off as if I'm joking – although I am not.

Once, the deceased father of the storekeeper in my small town appeared in my dream discussing the abilities of his son. He could be president if he wanted to. I wrote the dream and sent it to this man. I got a phone call from him thanking me and telling me he was on the verge of a huge change in his life and had wondered if his father would approve. Because of this dream encounter he felt he had the approval that was so important to him and would begin to build a chain of grocery stores. While I knew him, his chain grew to nine. I was operating a business of my own, at the time, and, after this, this man helped me in my business several times.

I have come to know that dreams of my daughter are almost always about something in her life that she has not yet decided to share with me. So, yes, I believe God and his angels, our angels, work in our dreams, for good or bad, to try to make our lives better. When my daughter's life is better, my life is better.

This is a good time to mention the collective unconscious and psychologist, Carl Jung. For those of you who may need an update on Carl Jung, he studied under Freud but left him and continued a less restrictive study of dreams. Best known, perhaps, was his study of what we call the collective unconsciousness. This would explain my being able to tap into my daughter's mind or the town grocer's mind.

Many of our dreams are right to the point but most have to be interpreted using symbols. This can lead us to the collective unconscious. Close to home, a house symbol is us, the basement being our own unconscious, things we have experienced in the past but forgotten. The first floor would be today. The upper floor is more spiritual in nature, leading to the collective unconscious.

Another common symbol is water. A small body of water, like a pond or pool, is you today. Are you drowning or having a good time in the water, fighting with someone over a water toy? A river may be your overall journey through life. The ocean is all of us together. Our knowing minds and/or spirits are flowing into each other. The waves that rock one person, rock a great many.

Within my current dream group is a lady named Katy who has studied Carl Jung extensively. She quotes him as saying that we carry within our consciousness a connection to the collective unconsciousness. Due to the creations of God that we are, we have access to this collective, and therefore have access to all that is, was and ever will be. This may explain how Abraham had this connection through his dreams, and so do we. There is no 'time' in the collective unconscious. We'll hear more from Katy and her Jungian thoughts as we go along. My interpretations are based on some Jung, my own experience and many other researchers. Only the person who had the dream will know the truth when it is spoken.

CHAPTER 3

Jacob

Genesis 25:vs 1 - 50

Jacob's life was an epic of dreams. He was the grandson of Abraham, the second son of Isaac. Songs have been written about his dreams including, "I Am Climbing Jacob's Ladder." To understand Jacob's dreams, it helps to understand Jacob. The same is true for us. When telling a dream in a group, there are many possible interpretations given but the one who had the dream will know exactly when the truth of the dream is mentioned. They know themselves best. Therefore, no one else in the group needs to know any more about the dreamer. The dreamer will get that 'ah-ha' feeling, like an awakening, and will probably think, why didn't I think of that? It is like we are too close to the subject to be able to see the truth for ourselves.

Jacob, according to the Bible, understood his dreams exactly. Ours are a bit more difficult. The society we live in is more complex. The angels give us the scenario that will hopefully make us change our minds. Sometimes the dreams are right on, but we might see them as referring to the wrong thing because we have a problem facing the truth. Or, like Rebecca, we try to push our own agenda once we know what something means.

Jacob was a twin. His brother's name was Esau. While still in the womb, their mother, Rebecca, was told by God, in a dream, that the baby born second (Jacob) would rule over the first. This was contrary to the culture of the times in which the oldest son inherited all. I would guess that Isaac (Jacob's father), having been almost sacrificed by his father, Abraham, did not have a close relationship with God. Isaac was more of a follower of the culture in which he lived, as was his son Esau. Jacob was swayed by his mother's dream for him. Although the boys came within minutes of each other, in their culture, the first-born would inherit everything. That seemed to go against what Rebecca was told in her dream.

Rebecca, like many of us, searched for a closer relationship to her creator but she wanted to hurry God's promise along. Rather than trust God to fulfill His promise, Rebecca set out to make sure this happened. When her husband, Isaac, lay on his death bed, Rebecca conspired with Jacob to deceive his father. The oldest son Esau was to be sent into a now blind Isaac and receive the blessings of the inheritance of all of Isaac's holdings. As it happened, Esau was working in a far field. Rebecca dressed Jacob in sheep skin to imitate Esau's hairy body. The father was deceived and gave the inheritance to Jacob by mistake. Esau was livid and promised to kill Jacob, so Rebecca sent Jacob to live with her brother, Laban.

Yes, it is shown in the Bible that women could learn about their children before they were born. But we women all know that, don't we? We even talk to them.

On the long trek to the house of Laban, Jacob prepared to spend one of the nights in the endless wilderness, as told in Genesis 28:vs12. He laid his head on a rock, immediately fell asleep and had a dream of a ladder reaching from Earth to Heaven with God's messengers going up and down.

This is another message for us all. God's angels do bring us messages in our dreams. Jacob honored God for the vision by building a monument to Him in that spot. Not because of this story but, similarly, it has always been my habit to try to find a way to honor God for each dream. If I could find a change to make in my life, my way of thinking, I would do it. If there was something I could draw or buy that represented something in the dream, I would do it. I'd spent so many years making promises to God and not following through (my diet, my exercising, my promises to the Grandmother who raised me) I felt I needed to keep declaring my intent to follow his message.

The other lesson is the sight of the angels coming down to us and returning to Heaven, our connection with our creator. These are the angels who care for us. We must not miss out on the wisdom our angels, guides and other loved ones bring to us. I've come to know that they know everything about us and love us still, and always want the best for us.

Another way of looking at the ladder dream is that there is a Heaven, life is bigger than ourselves. Plus,

Heaven is not that far away. We can make an easy transition when the time comes.

Jacob's mother had been told Jacob was special but still Jacob suffered. He was thrown out of his home, left his beloved mother and traveled across all kinds of land, hoping he'd find his uncle, Laban, whom he'd never met. Also, he worried if his uncle would even give him a home if he found him. He finally came upon a well and the most beautiful girl he had ever seen. He immediately fell in love. Upon inquiring if she knew of a man named Laban, he learned she was Laban's daughter and followed her home. Laban said Jacob could stay and work for seven years at which time he and Rachel could be married, even though she was the younger of two daughters and the custom was that the older daughter was to marry first.

Jacob worked diligently for seven years, the wedding took place but when the bride was unveiled, it was not Rachel, but her sister, Leah. Jacob had been tricked. Laban then said, if you stay seven more years, you may also marry Rachel. Jacob worked hard, grew himself a herd of cattle, sheep and other live stock. So wonderful were they, that Laban became jealous and accused Jacob of stealing from him. Jacob married Rachel, took his holdings and left Laban's land.

Jacob, in Genesis 31, was being cheated at every turn by his father-in-law, Laban. Laban was jealous of Jacob's success in raising not only striped and spotted goats and sheep but jealous of his increasing family and servants as well. Laban was making Jacob's life miserable. God came in a dream during breeding season, while Jacob slept in a field with his herd. Jacob tells about the dream: "The angel of God called to me in the dream, 'Jacob.' I answered, 'here I am.' And He said 'Look up and see all the male goats mating with the flock are streaked, speckled or spotted, for I have seen all of what Laban has been doing to you. I am the God of Bethel, where you anointed a pillar and where you made a vow to me. Now leave this land at once and go back to your native land."

With the negative atmosphere, the constant disagreements, Laban was keeping Jacob from his destiny. In his dreams and in his life, God was compensating Jacob for his troubles by showing him where, when, and how to proceed with his life.

But, you ask, would he give you a place to live, a domain in which to be the master? We don't know how many miracles God and his angels are inclined to grant. My thoughts are that it depends on what He perceives is His true need of us. Make yourself available through your dreams and meditations.

God desires our spiritual growth, not increased material possessions. If something is necessary for our spiritual-emotional growth, God will provide it. If we are not aware of our dreams, a sudden change in our lives may seem negative. Perhaps we are not in the habit of trusting God. By catching the message, first in our dreams, the negative quality will disappear.

If this was my dream, the mating of the animals might be speaking of something I know how to do but do not often get a chance to do. Evidently there was something special about spotted animals and Laban often claimed Jacob's spotted lambs as his. Is someone stealing the gift I got from God? Has someone said what I desire is foolish? Have we been told little girls are to be seen and not heard? Do we talk of our ideas and then see someone else do them? Sometimes we need freedom and courage to do what we want to do. This is what this dream might be telling me if I had a similar one today.

For Jacob's own good, God is asking him to make a huge change in his life, to take a chance. The message of your dreams may be similar. It could be pushing you to change where you live, how you work or work out, your relationships, how you think about yourself, or your attitudes on things, for example.

Jacob headed back to his old home, hoping to impress his mother and brother with his big family and other holdings. Perhaps they would forgive him and let him back into the family. Along the way, riders approached and warned Jacob that his brother was approaching from the other direction with a great army, intent on killing him. Jacob feared for himself and his family and sent his family, servants and livestock across the river while he waited alone to meet his brother. He prayed as he lay down to sleep that night.

In his dream, Jacob was set upon by a huge monster and they wrestled. Jacob was fed up with being the underdog, with everyone pushing him around, and fought like he'd never fought before. All night they fought. Finally, the monster had enough and asked to stop fighting. Jacob said only if the monster blessed him with a wonderful gift. The monster then revealed that he was an emissary of God, sent to tell Jacob that his name was now Israel and he would be the father of nations because he had wrestled with both man and God and won both times.

Our Jungian specialist, Katy, would remind us that the 'monster' comes from our shadow side, our repressed side. There is a whole book on this subject. It can represent the reasons we don't love ourselves. It can be a talent we never pursued, perhaps a line of work we should have tackled. Jacob decided to make peace with his shadow side. The story is telling us we can do that also.

A woman, in a class on dream interpretation that I was teaching, told of a recurring dream she's had most of her life. In her dream she'd be doing something, turn around, and there was a strange man. He scared her. Actually, he was a visitor from her shadow side (a side of ourselves we've buried). An opportunity was there now for her to turn and allow that unused part of herself into her life. She could go back into the dream and ask what he wanted.

It could just as well have been a monster instead of a strange man. The committee in Heaven who sends us our dreams decides on the importance of the message in our life and wonder how we will react. Will she turn easily and not need a monster to chase her, to make her desperate? She could turn and demand a gift from him like Jacob did. She may then realize something important that has been missing from her life.

There is another lesson in the dream of Jacob and the monster. Jacob purposely turned on the monster. He intended to change the end of the dream no matter what it took. This borders on a kind of dream action present day researchers call lucid dreaming. You are aware and in charge enough in your dream state to interact with the story.

I often tell people who have a bad experience in a dream but want to know the message to go back to bed, put a note under your pillow about your intentions, and think about that dream as you fall asleep. You can drift off to sleep with this story line in your head and direct the action to a more favorable outcome. Is this negating God's wishes for you? I don't think so. The fact that you are studying the dream tells God you want to know His message. Your outcome may hold a clue to the message. Try to carry this forward in your life as well. Jacob was not going to be beat by anyone else, period!

Don't forget the part about asking for a gift. The answer may show up in a few days. Live in a state of expectation, open to all opportunities.

Feeling magnanimous with his gift, Jacob changed his mind and sent many animals, food and servants to Esau as a peace offering. Esau and Jacob met with open arms of love. Jacob built an altar to God to honor the dream. When we embrace the negative thoughts and feelings within us we heal our inner wounds better and become more whole. Don't forget the 'altering' part.

A similar thing happened to me. I had a recurring problem for which I turned to God. He led me back in time to each time I'd experienced a similar set of circumstances, bringing on a great angry, physically sick, and emotional hurt in me. I was led back to the original time when the seed for this had been planted and was able to forgive the people involved (because I knew then that they did not know any better) and then came back up through the years seeing myself over-reacting to each similar situation. I never had to apologize. My attitude miraculously changed, and people accepted me differently.

Can you imagine dreaming of wrestling with a monster? It could get very frightening. Talk of nightmares! Jacob got angry with the monster and demanded a gift. Suppose that in your waking life, you are wrestling with a problem that seems to have the best of you, and you are at your wits end. In your dreams you get this monster beating you to the ground. That seems like enough to drive anyone into depression, being forced to accept what you seemingly can't fight. Here is where we need to turn towards the villain in our nightmares and ask what he wants from us.

Know that the monster of your dreams is a part of you, the part of yourself searching for a different outcome. Call it the spark of God inside us all. It wants you to get angry and end the whole thing. Does it mean for you to do something rash? No. It most likely wants to change your view about the path you are on. A change of attitude can make all the difference. Go back into that dream and face the monster and ask, 'what do you want of me? The real answer will change your outlook, give you a set of answers much better than what you are living. As some wise people say, it is not what they do to me that matters, but rather, how I react to what they do to me.

I have used this dream a few times to illustrate the meaning of another person's dream. To me, it means that Jacob had reached the end of his patience and was not about to be taken advantage of anymore. Occasionally,

I've run into people who have had a similar dream. I ask them to look at where in their life they need to finally take charge. Each time, the dreamer then knew exactly what the dream meant, and took steps to right the wrongs in their lives. God, in their dreams, gave them the strength they didn't have before.

From Jacob's dreams I got the idea of honoring each dream, whether I understood it or not. It's like saying, "I'm listening and ready to do whatever you ask." I instinctively knew God would only ask me to do what is right for this world, what is good. The angels ascending and descending the ladders bring the messages we receive in our dreams. What have we missed? It is never too late. As the old saying goes, 'It's better late than never.'

A lady I once counseled about arthritis began talking of a recurring dream she was suffering from regularly. In the dream, a man chased her. She ran, clutching her purse. My reaction was to go back into the dream (you can do this) and give him the purse. It is an item that men never use. Like them, we can use our pockets. Go back into the dream, give him the purse and ask him what he wants of you?

She suddenly remembered that her son had built a room onto his house several years ago for her to move into in her old age. She instinctively knew that this was what her dream was about, and she was ready to make the move. The purse represented the independence she thought she would be giving up. Later, I received thank you notes from both her and her son. It was all in her dream and the nightmare was over.

My own nightmares were tied to a lack of a feeling of

self-worth. I did not realize that was a problem of mine but as I worked with the dreams I gradually changed my opinion of myself, especially of what I could do. I changed my opinion of those who put me down. Before, I had believed them. As I gained wisdom the nightmares disappeared. Besides that, opportunities came to do things I'd had no idea I could do. Thank you, God!

If you are suffering nightmares at night and stress during your waking hours, your dreams hold the answer to both. Someone a lot older and smarter than you, someone who knows all about you and loves you anyway, wants the best for you. The angels, God, are trying to make your life better, more interesting, healthier, prosperous, fun, and more. We each have a path, and if we are on the wrong path, or neglecting our path, we will be unhappy. Dreams (nightmares especially) will bring you step-by-step in the right direction for you. The reward is wonderful, definitely worth living for.

Jacob's reward was to become the father of the nation known as Israel.

My reward was that I became more self-confident which enabled me to find more suitable employment, and, most importantly, led me into my dream study work.

From Jungian Katy we hear that Jung argued that spiritual and emotional work leads to who we really are, or 'individuation.' That is a word to think on. We each were put here by God to fulfill a part in the script of life. Raymond Moody, writer and researcher of the book, "Life After Life," called this a post we are meant to fill. We can grow into this unique identity, dreamed of by God. Like Jacob, God has great plans for each of us.

CHAPTER 4

Joseph

Joseph was the youngest son of Jacob and he was also Jacobs' favorite. You may recall the story of Joseph and the coat of many colors that his father had made just for him. His several older brothers were jealous and did not like Joseph very much. This is told in Genesis 37:3. Joseph was a prolific dreamer. In Genesis 37:5, "Joseph had a dream and when he told it to his brothers, they hated him even more. He said to them. 'Listen to this dream I had: We were binding sheaves of grain out in the field when suddenly my sheaf rose and stood upright, while your sheaves gathered around mine and bowed down to it." Verse 8, "His brothers said to him, 'Do you intend to reign over us?' And they hated him all the more because of his dream and what he said."

We all get predictions in our dreams. Seldom are they as great as this, but you never know. What is great to you may be as little as the prediction of a visit from a friend you haven't seen in a while. I record my dreams, as best I can, and then re-read them every few months.

I find it amazing how the dreams have predicted the events of my life.

In verse nine Joseph had another dream that he told to his brothers." Listen," he said," I had another dream, and this time the sun and moon and eleven stars bowed down to me." The brothers must have disliked him for his story-telling that showed not only their father, but a king as well, showing him favoritism.

When he told his father his dream, his father lovingly rebuked him.

Lesson one is that we all need someone to talk to about our dreams. Second is to be very careful who you chose. Then there may be times when there's no one to share with but your journal. It is all you have. The third and greatest lesson is what God told Joseph. He will tell us our future.

Some people might be jealous or think you are bragging about something you say you can do that they can't. There is no reason for anyone to be jealous; it is an ability we all have. The reaping of the promise depends on the effort you devote to your dreams. So many people have never given a thought to dreams. For this book, I'd like to take each dream as if it came to me, or you, and find other possible meanings that would hold relevance in today's world.

Our Jungian fan, Katy, tells us the sheaves and the stars are images for the fractured masculine that must be integrated into Joseph's life for him to be whole. The fractured masculine means the male side of us is not yet whole. It has not yet come together to present a complete picture of who we are meant to be. This can be found in both a male and a female. If it was my dream it probably would be pointing to something in my work life and its future – reach for the stars.

Joseph is young. His male spiritual side has not grown to maturity yet. Reading Jung, you'll see that we must reach a wholeness of self; an individuation of self. We need to grow to become who God meant us to be. Joseph's journey in the rest of his story is to further this integration. It will bring him to be the person he is meant to be. For those not familiar with Jung's teachings, we each, male and female, have both masculine and feminine energies within us. The ideal is to find a balance between them.

If it was my dream, the sheaves might represent a responsibility I have. Then again, young children at that time did share a responsibility. Perhaps I need to take something into my life and bind it tighter to me before I lose it. Get to work. Claim it.

Sheaves are cut from roots I've planted months ago. Maybe it is time to let them go. Maybe I will soon reap a reward for all my work. It may simply be a pat on the back as in 'good job.'

The sun, moon, and stars bowing to me might be saying the same thing but, I think, also, this is between God and me. I should continue to do the same as I have been doing, knowing it is right. I'll go quietly about my business and await instructions from my dreams.

To continue Joseph's story, his brothers conspired to kill him. They buried him alive in a pit but then hauled him out and sold him to traders headed for Egypt. They marked his famous coat with goat's blood and told his father he was dead. Joseph became a slave, then ended up in jail. He worked hard in prison. Besides, he interpreted dreams for others and became friends with his superiors.

During this same time, the King of Egypt's cupbearer and baker were also prisoners because they had displeased the king. They came to be assigned into Joseph's custody. While there, they each had a dream, separate dreams, on the same night.

There are a couple of things to be learned here. First, and most important, is that you don't have to be a special person to have dreams. Some would argue that we are all special in our own way. Specialness is not the criteria of whether you remember your dreams or not, or whether you are a thief (because these men were servants and prisoners). It doesn't seem to matter what your station in life is for you to have meaningful dreams.

My book "Prison Dreams" is based on my prison ministry. The stories are all prisoner's dreams and the reactions they had upon studying them. All are very thought provoking.

Katy says our unconscious brings forth the images to express the feelings we are experiencing in our waking life, therefore attempting to help us move toward spiritual wholeness. What would the symbol of a playful puppy mean in your dreams? The best is yet to come? Enjoy the now?

Back to Joseph's baker and servant. They each reported dreams about what they did for a living. We have a saying in dream circles that dreams use what we know to teach us what we don't know. What we did for a living is common in our dreams. Look for the small, unusual twist. A postman will dream of sorting mail, going door to door. When you think of all the people on this planet, God and His angels are surely busy and spend a lot of time with our dreams. They need to use symbols familiar to us. Dreams use what we've lived, with a small twist, in hopes of convincing us to take a different path, take another look at decisions we are about to make, prepare us for a difficult happening that will improve our lives.

Next is the interpretation of the dreams. When they asked Joseph while he was in prison for an interpretation, he answered in Gen.40:8, "Do not interpretations belong to God?" In dream groups we each tell about what your dream may mean to us if we'd had it. You, the dreamer, will get that "ah-ha" feeling when the truth is told. The dream is truly between you and your creator. It helps to have others of like mind jog our thoughts. Joseph was only guessing, but, thanks to his many years of practice, he was right on.

The rest of the dreams of the king's servants show us the interpretation. The cupbearers dream told in verse nine, "In my dream I saw a vine in front of me, and on the vine were three branches. As soon as it budded, it blossomed, and its clusters ripened into grapes. Pharaoh's cup was in my hand and I took the grapes, squeezed them into Pharaoh's cup and put the cup in his hand."

Verse 12; "This is what it means," Joseph said to him. "The three branches are three days. Within three days Pharaoh will lift up your head and restore you to your position, and you will put Pharaoh's cup in his hand, just as you used to do when you were his cupbearer." I question why he should have his old job back. My guess is that he served his master well. Joseph goes on to try to exact a promise from this man to tell the pharaoh about his ability to dream interpret dreams, but in the long run, his service is forgotten.

If anyone should ever have appreciated having a dream interpreted, it should have been this man, as it is a correct interpretation and relieved him greatly. If it was my dream, I might start by drawing a picture of a vine and the three branches of the vine which pass on to form a cluster of beautiful flowers that turn into grapes and ends up as wine pouring into a cup for the Pharaoh. Everything in the dream is alive and growing, prospering, and nourishing.

If it was my dream, it might be a promise of good things to come, whether I work for a pharaoh, am a writer, or even work in the water works department. That opens a new thought. Maybe something is going wrong at the water works department (my emotions) and needs my tender care to clean unnecessary weeds out of my life.

It all depends on the life you are living. The three branches, or three of anything, can refer to the Trinity, a message from God. I love the opportunity to nourish others, as the healthy grapes would do. Then, again, perhaps I'm being warned of someone in my circle of friends drinking too much, maybe even me. The person in my dream circle, having the dream, knows the truth by that "ah-ha" feeling God will give him or her.

Katy reminds us that we are all connected to God. Jung calls this a realization of the Self, capitol 'S' or God within us. Our growth is dependent on our consciously connecting to the Self, and dreams will show the way for us to do this.

The baker, however has quite a different dream. "I had a dream: On my head were three baskets. In the top basket were all kinds of baked goods for Pharaoh, but birds were eating them out of the basket on my head." Again, Joseph saw the three baskets (dead, not growing) holding baked goods that because of his positioning of them on his head allowed birds to eat their contents, leaving nothing for the Pharaoh. This might be a bad job in the Pharaoh's eyes. Joseph interpreted that he would be dead in three days, hung from a tree, food for the birds. The baskets hold nothing and perhaps Joseph saw this as the man, himself. We often work with the idea that every person and everything in a dream is a part of us. This baker was an empty basket – dead. He used to bring bread to the Pharaoh, but he has let it all slip away with his present lifestyle. There is nothing left to pass on to his master.

If it was anyone else's dream, the empty baskets on the head might be pointing to a life of head more than heart. The birds are very spiritual. The fact that they were trying to feed out of empty baskets, or gathering crumbs, may be telling the dreamer to prepare his spiritual life. His soul, symbolized by the birds, may be preparing for a spiritual journey. If it was your dream, look where you might make changes, become a gift to the world.

The Pharaoh would see future nourishment with the cupbearer but not the baker and decided their fates accordingly. Your own death seen in a dream usually means a change is coming, or should come, I've seen my own death many times and I'm still here.

Katy says that Jung taught that we will not dream of our own death directly. The dream of the baker supports the use of images for our death. Katy says she believes it is because our soul, or self, will never die. This is an argument for everlasting life or life beyond the passage we know as death. Can we, do we come back, is a story for another time. My own dreams have given me glimpses of this. I'm a believer.

Interpreting another's dreams is not bad so long as the feeling of truth is left to the dreamer. Suggest, do not tell the meaning of a dream as you see it. Suggesting many possibilities is very helpful to the dreamer, and it opens your own mind to more than one possible truth. God will tell the dreamer when the right interpretation is mentioned. Understanding your dream can bring an end to that kind of dream, it need not become a nightmare, and your life will change for the better. Your path of life will come closer to what it is meant to be, who you were meant to be. If you were that baker, you might have saved your own life by finally turning to the spiritual side of life; by starting a conversation with God.

Since only the top basket of the three held bread, essential to our lives in more than one way, I might have gone back into the dream and eliminated the bottom two empty baskets. Why carry empty baggage around? Then I would contemplate, where in my life could I eliminate one or two burdens? Where in my life could I get by with carrying one dream of a future, take one opportunity and lose the bottom two empty baskets that are causing me nothing but worry, stress?

We can learn a lot from these dreams in the Bible.

Back to the Bible, two years have passed with Joseph in prison in Egypt. The Pharaoh has two dreams in the same night. Asking around, he finally learns of Joseph's ability to interpret dreams and consults with him. Genesis, Chapter 41, begins the story of the dream of the seven healthy, fat cows that come out of the river followed by seven ugly, gaunt cows. The Pharaoh wakes up, goes back to sleep and dreams of seven heads of grain, healthy and good, followed by seven heads of thin, scorched by the wind, heads of grain.

When God has a message for you and you do not get it the first time, a different story with the same theme will come in future nights, eventually becoming stronger and scarier. If it was my dream, I might worry about my health, about the fact that the things I nourish my body with are failing me. But, thank God, I do not have the responsibilities of a pharaoh.

Joseph interprets the two dreams as seven years of abundance followed by seven very tough years for the Pharaoh's world. The Pharaoh sees the wisdom of Joseph's words and puts him in charge of all of Egypt, second to no one except the pharaoh, himself. Joseph stockpiles the food during the next seven years of plenty and has plenty of food and grain to sell and feed not only to the Egyptians but others as well. Can you see the fulfillment of Joseph's childhood dreams? Later on in the story, his brothers do indeed bow down and beg for food from him.

What's to learn from this besides how to manage your assets? People believe Joseph had direct access to God. Joseph had been dealing with dreams since his early childhood while most others, much like today, can't spend the time to learn how. I find in my dream groups that some people have a natural ability and others need to spend time and effort learning to interpret dreams, much like the people surrounding the pharaoh who tried. The others do learn to understand the dreams and can become very good at it. So, where does that leave us as far as the belief that God is talking to us?

Our creator never meant to lose touch with us. He gave us all the power of dreams. If you believe in the many mentions of dreams in the Bible, you should want to study and learn to understand the emotional and spiritual language of your dreams, as it says in the Bible. Whether it is God, directly, speaking to us, a committee of loving spirits, our personal angels, or at times all three; we have dreams that tell us all kinds of good things, and they warn us of the bad. Someone older and wiser than we are, someone who knows all about us and loves us still and wants the best for us, our health, our finances, our joy; that someone speaks to us in our dreams.

Katy, our Jungian specialist, and also a Catholic Priest, says that God has a part for each unique individual to play in the evolution of human consciousness and spirituality.

We could possibly avoid some of the results of the various disasters if we paid attention to our dreams like

Joseph and the Pharaoh did. That is what Genesis 41 is telling us. Some people believe the disasters come to teach us lessons. Some of us learn of future problems by writing our dreams and therefore avoiding disasters. Some of us learn those lessons, after the fact. Some learn for a while during the turmoil, then forget as time goes by.

Few of us continue the humanitarian aspects of life for very long after a disaster. We go back to thinking and feeling about those less fortunate than ourselves the same way as we did before the storm, earthquake, or whatever it was that the disaster was supposed to teach us.

Perhaps, though, the ultimate lesson is to monitor our dreams for the predictions they bring us, so we can begin the clean-up or even possibly avoid disaster before it happens.

Katy, our Jungian expert, says that a physical event is always signaled by an emotional/spiritual change within ourselves, usually seen first in dreams. Joseph's emotional/spiritual experience moves him to go to Egypt, a "new foreign" position for him and his family. Hmmmm. Have you recently been moved to a "new foreign" position in your life?

Toward the end of Genesis, Chapter 46, Joseph had prospered and caused all of Egypt to turn to him for guidance. This included his brothers, although they did not recognize him, Joseph knew them immediately. He asked to be reunited with his youngest brother and his beloved father, Jacob, who all these years thought Joseph was dead. In Chapter 46; verse 2 "God spoke to Israel (Jacob) in a vision of the night and said, "Jacob, Jacob." Jacob answered "Here I am." And God said, "I am God, the God of your father; do not fear to go down to Egypt, for I will make you a great nation there." He added that his long lost son, Joseph, would be there.

Jacob loaded all his belongings and people and went.

If you had a dream telling you to do something that big, would you? We often have dreams but no way of knowing who is talking to us. I try always to honor God in each dream. If there is a clear direction, I do my best to follow it. I always give thanks to God for a night's dreams remembered, even though the meaning may not yet be clear.

My faith tells me God would never tell me to hurt myself or someone else. If I get a bad image, I turn it around, look at the opposite of the action. Many wonderful results have come from this. May God bless you likewise.

CHAPTER 5

Exodus, Leviticus, and Numbers

The next two books of the Bible are free of dreams. The next, Numbers, does not mention them until the twelfth chapter, verse six. The Lord is speaking, according to the author of Numbers. He said, "When a prophet of the Lord is among you, I reveal myself to him in visions, I speak to him in dreams. This is not true of my servant Moses; he is faithful in all my house. With him, I speak face-to-face, clearly and not in riddles, he sees the form of the Lord.

Do you take the Bible seriously? If you do, this seems a clear directive to study your dreams! Prophets are few these days. I believe you do not have to be a prophet. In the New Testament, because Jesus says we can do as he does and even more. Don't let the religious groups who do not believe in dreams sway you.

The statement from the Bible quoted above makes me wonder. Can we hope to see God some day? Can we hope to converse with him face-to-face as Moses did? The dreams are made possible by God. I feel the direct orders I have been given, the writings on the wall, are directly from Him. God, angels, whatever committees are set up in Heaven to handle such things are under the direction of God. All is one.

Moses was not a prophet. He had been given many gifts that astonished him and the people around him, and those of us reading the Bible are still filled with surprise at his dreams. There were gifts such as turning a walking stick into a snake and then back into a stick. Moses is a strong leader and his reign is filled with new laws. Through the many years of his reign, however, Moses' people were seldom satisfied, and the Lord suffered with them, and wondered how to handle them.

I'll bet He wonders how to handle us.

I find it interesting that in Numbers, Chapter 12: verse 6, he says he will talk to Moses clearly, not in riddles. I've often been frustrated and heard other people express frustration over the need to interpret our dreams. Talk about riddles! Some dreams come through very clearly, and at times a clear sentence will come through with directions pertaining to whatever is important in your life.

Then other dreams come to change our attitude about something. These quite often are the dreams that need interpreting. They are stories that play with our emotions. What would it take to get you to go with a second choice, or a third choice you would never have known existed? When faced with a problem, I'd ask God before going to sleep, which way to go, option one or option two, and then I had a dream about a third choice I'd never thought of. If you believed someone older, wiser and loving wanted to change the way you felt about something, you very well might take a different path. You feel differently about the subject. First of all, you need to be open to the advice you get in your dreams and keep a pad and pen next to your bed, so you don't miss a dream that once understood, could change your life.

In a dream, I was told that after this earthly life, I would serve on a committee that gives dreams to people on earth. I worry if I understand human nature enough to have any idea what it would take to change their minds about something. Serving on a committee of souls trying to mold the thoughts and feelings of people on earth brings me some comfort. I don't want to miss this chance of service in the afterlife. This is a beautiful outlook of continuous hope.

It is all about seeing a situation from various views. The views could convince the person to choose differently. If you worry about your afterlife, ask God.

When I began my serious dream study, it took only a year to erase rheumatoid arthritis from my blood stream. It took following the dreams as closely as I could. My relationships changed, my vocation certainly changed. I did not grow up wanting to do dream work, I didn't even know what dreams were. I saw in the dreams different ways to see things. My first thoughts, or ego thoughts, did not suit me after I saw other ways of viewing a situation shown me in my dreams.

Often you think you are simply reliving something in your dream that happened in your life. Rev. Jeremy

Taylor (an Episcopal dream researcher) told us that the dreams use what you know to teach you what you don't know. Think on that.

I had a male friend who was a hospital administrator for most of his adult life. The dreams he told in our dream circle often had him back in that hospital, walking the same halls and rooms, even being in the parking garage. He had to look at the inconsistencies, the twists, compare them to whatever was going on in his life now to find the message. Dreams use what you know to teach you what you don't know. If you delivered mail for a living, walking a city block, house to house, business to business, this is where your message may be hidden. The dream messengers, the Lord, want you to follow your own truths, make your own choices, with just a little push from above.

Unlike the people of Moses time, who were asked to follow blindly, most of us have the power of choice. Call it free will. Let us make the best choices we can.

CHAPTER 6

Deuteronomy 13:1

"If a prophet, or one who foretells by dreams, appears among you and announces to you a miraculous sign or wonder, and if the sign or wonder of which he has spoken takes place, and he says, 'Let us follow other gods and let us worship them, you must not listen to the words of that prophet or dreamer."

This is, perhaps, the most misunderstood passage in the Bible. If it weren't for the 134 dreams, the Bible would be very thin. Some people take this to mean to stay away from dreams altogether. Nowhere in the Bible does it say to not follow your own dreams, or not to listen for your creator's voice. It says the opposite in several places.

The key in this passage is the phrase, "And he says, let us follow other gods and let us worship them." That comes naturally to a lot of us a lot of the time and hopefully this will change.

This verse has been thrown in my face by people who've heard of it but not taken the time to read the Bible themselves. I went back to the beginning of the Book of

Deuteronomy and read every word again to get a feel for whatever was going on. Moses, at this point, is reaching the end of his years and must pass his knowledge of the laws onto the leaders taking his place. I can understand him saying something that would encourage them to get their own messages from God, and not use an in-between person. Nowhere does it say to not follow your <u>own</u> dreams.

Other Biblical scholars have said this book was translated from Arabic to Spanish by the translator, Jerome. It is said that he made a mistake in the word 'dream'. He said the reference to the word dream was originally to be 'fortune teller'. Jerome is credited with ten mistakes. The Bible has been translated many times, not only to change the language but also to change the meaning, which is easily shown by the many translations on the market today. We shall touch on the ancient texts later in this book. The rest of Deuteronomy is about the many laws God passed through Moses, including the Ten Commandments.

After Moses died, Joshua was given commands by God. He followed the rules and God helped him conquer a lot of the land the Israelites had been promised.

I have to say, this whole story, maybe a lot of the Bible, could be interpreted as relating to our own lives. If we learn to hear the word of God through our dreams and meditations, and then follow that Word, God will grant us great things in life.

After the reign of Joshua, the people became friendly with the people they overcame, and that friendship led them to follow other gods. This brings us to the book of Judges and the rule of Gideon. Although God spoke directly to Gideon, as He did to Moses, Gideon was hard to convince that he was really hearing from God. Gideon asked for signs that what he was thinking was truly from God. When he was convinced, he often bargained with God. (Perhaps this sounds a little like us?)

My own initial experience of spirituality was so powerful I just knew only God could be helping me. When things came and frightened me, as also happened with a couple of the inmates in my dream class, we pleaded with God to take away the bad things of our dreams (I call them demons) and He did. You will find the whole story about this in my book, "Prison Dreams."

Katy, again from her Jungian perspective, reminds us not to let others tell us the meaning of our dreams. Only take suggestions. Only the dreamer knows the true meaning of the dream, although it may take several dreams to finally get the message across. Katy asks who is the God of our understanding? She says, we each have a unique relationship with our Creator. First the dream is for us, about our challenges, choices, and feelings. These dreams arise from our personal unconscious, our anxieties with our path in life. Secondly, dream images may come from the collective unconscious (the unconscious belonging to the world). These bring symbols such as the father, mother, babies, house, – something we all share. Therefore, the dreams have connections with other people and/or knowledge beyond our conscious understanding of a situation until it is made known to us.

Katy has added this to my book, but my personal experience says she is right on.

CHAPTER 7

Judges 7:13

The action in this passage is very similar to the better-known story of Sodom and Gomorrah. God needs to weed out the people who do not bring honor to his name. In Sodom and Gomorrah, Abraham is begging God to save a community. "If I can find ten honorable people will you still destroy the community?" The next morning, a group of angels are accosted on their way into town and all deals are off. The towns are wiped out.

In Judges, the story concerns God and Gideon. There is much negotiating as Gideon does not want to go to war. God convinces him to take one trusted person with him and scout the enemy camp during the night. The decision is left up to Gideon, but the seed is planted. In Judges 7:13, "Gideon arrived just as a man (an enemy) was telling a friend his dream. 'I had a dream,' he was saying. A round loaf of barley bread came tumbling into the Midianite camp. It struck the tent with such a force that the tent overturned and collapsed.' Judge 7:14, "His friend responded,' This can be nothing other than the sword of Gideon, son of Joash, the Israelite. God has given the Midianites and the whole camp into his hands.

Judges Chapter 7, verse 15 says, "When Gideon heard the dream and its interpretation, he worshiped God. He returned to the camp of Israel and called out. 'Get up! The Lord has given the Midianite camp into your hands."

The writers of the Bible are proving that God has a hand in everything. We often see something familiar. The dream and its interpretation were very familiar to Gideon and he knew when the very same words were repeated through someone else's dream that God was re-emphasizing His message.

If I was Gideon, today, I believe I'd be having a feeling of Déjà Vu. This happens to most of us some time in our life, that we walk into a room or a situation and feel that we've been there before. Perhaps we've been shown it in our dreams. If this is the way things are supposed to work, if people were to take heed of their dreams, would much of the fighting in this world never happen?

There is a book titled, "The Third Reich of Dreams," written mostly in the 1930s before World War II started. The author, a German woman named Charlotte Beradt, a journalist, was able to gather hundreds of dreams. Often the people to whom she spoke about such things did not even know she was keeping a journal of them. The person who wrote the introduction saw in the telling of the dreams that the Nazis could reach into our dreams and scare us into submission. Charlotte Beradt escaped to England in 1940 and eventually to the US where she published her book in 1966.

I see something different when I read the book. I see the horror coming to the average German, but I also see an opportunity to change things. I believe Ms. Beradt did also, which would explain her escape to England.

We can know the future from our dreams. It is too bad we lost our belief in this ability for communication with our creator for so long. In my work with dream groups, I find hope as more and more people become interested in learning what their dreams are telling them.

One woman in my prison dream group told of a dream where she is on the beach, fighting off the advances of an old toothless shark in an attempt to save her friends. I suggested this is how she sees herself, as a shark, picking on the weaker when she finds them. She agreed. The dream showed her new natural tendencies were to save them.

A year of prison classes went by with her trying to learn the right way to live, GED classes, parenting classes, cooking, religion, and other things. A year later her dream had her walking along the beach, picking up shark's teeth. She met me at the gate, excited to tell me of the dream we both remembered. She was regaining her strength.

Back to Gideon, in the beginning of the story, it seems as though Gideon is talking directly to God. Why, then, did he not believe him? He believed the synchronicity when he heard another person tell his dream and the interpretation so very similar to what he'd experienced. Then he knew God was God and God was serious. We may be getting messages each night in our dreams and are doubting they are from God. This is where faith, belief and finally, "knowing," come into play.

The lesson in the dream we spoke of earlier, is the ball of barley rolling down the hill to crush the camp. How would you feel if a huge ball of something was about to run over you and there was no way of getting out of the way? Pretty scary.

Are you in the wrong place in life? Bread, to me, means 'manna' which is a gift from God. If you or I had a similar dream, it might very well mean there is something in our life about to be rolled flat to make room for God's purpose. I believe it is a spiritual thing, or could be a belief or attitude, because of the word bread. It could be a warning of change, or maybe a gift from God.

CHAPTER 8

1 Samuel

1 Samuel 3:vs5: Samuel was born to a woman desperate for a child. During this time, Eli was God's representative and once every year, the people would go to Eli and sacrifice grains and animals. Eli saw this woman (Hannah) crying and praying so he asked God to grant her wish. She became pregnant and gave the boy child to Eli to grow up as a man of God. She had several children after that.

I can't help but interpret – be careful what you wish for. This woman was so grateful, she asked Eli to raise the child. She wanted the best for her child. The child was named Samuel.

Eli's own sons were thieves, taking from the sacrificial goods brought by the people.

Samuel remained pure of heart, true to Eli's guidance. One night, God called Samuel's name as he slept. Samuel thought it was Eli and ran to him. It happened again. The third time, Eli figured out that God must be calling to Samuel in his dream and told Samuel to go back to sleep and, upon hearing his name called again say, "I am Samuel, God, what can I do for you?"

1 Samuel, Chapter 3, verse 11, it reads, "The Lord said to Samuel: See, I am about to do something in Israel that will make the ears of everyone who hears of it tingle.

At that time, I will carry out against Eli everything I spoke against his family – from beginning to end. For I told him that I would judge his family forever because of the sin he knew about; his sons made themselves contemptible, and he failed to restrain them. Therefore, I swore to the house of Eli, the guilt of Eli's house will never be atoned for by sacrifice or offering."

Samuel was being given a prediction of something to happen against the family who raised him. Is it possible that you might be given a prediction of some awful thing happening in the future to someone you know?

Yes, it happens, but remember, God cares about you and wants to forewarn you to make the shock less for you. The worst thing for the health of our bodies is stress. Also, in the case of a death, every group needs one strong person to lean on and you have the chance to be that strong person.

There are few dreams between Genesis and 1st Samuel. We go through the books of Exodus, Leviticus, Numbers, Deuteronomy, Joshua, Judges, and Ruth. In Exodus, Moses warns against dreamers and seers. There are a couple of reasons given by Bible scholars as to why Moses is quoted as saying what he did. Some say Jerome, a Bible translator, made ten mistakes, but my own personal belief is that Moses wanted people to rely on their own connection with God. Nowhere in the Bible does it say not to follow your <u>own</u> dreams.

After Moses death there was at first a series of kings and then, for a long time, no kings or central leaders. The people who had based their lives on God's leadership began turning to other kings. In these books of the Bible are a series of wars. Sounds like today in the Middle East. Using symbols and metaphors, I find the way our personal lives often go from one stressful event to another.

It pleased me that in 1 Samuel 28, Saul, who had banished all seers and dreamers from his land, suddenly saw a need for a medium who could help him get advice from the Lord to save his country. Remind you of the atheist in the foxhole? Many of our own leaders seem to have lost the ability to hear God's voice.

In Chapter 28; verse 4, it is written; "The Philistines assembled and came and set up camp at Shunem, while Saul gathered all the Israelites and set up camp at Gilboa. When Saul saw the Philistine army, he was afraid: terror filled his heart. He inquired of the Lord, but the Lord did not answer him by dreams or prophets."

There is a time when we need God. Again, in verse 11 Saul says, "God has turned away from me. He no longer answers me by prophets or by dreams."

It is not God who turns away from us. It is we who do the turning. We must learn to remember our dreams, keep the doors of communication with God open.

Saul was unable to listen to his dreams because it is something we should practice continuously. When we are emotionally and physically stressed, mentally ill, or have addictions, we will have to focus on healing.

Our dreams may reveal a path for our healing. Because of Saul's circumstances, he could not choose a healthy path forward without knowing how to listen to God in his dreams.

Saul turned first to his dreams. Can you ask a question and get an answer? Have you ever gone to sleep with a deep worry on your mind and awakened the next morning with the answer? It happens.

When I have had health problems like headaches or urinary tract infections, I put a note to God under my pillow, having prayed about it first, and received the answer for a cure in my dreams. Try it. If at first you don't succeed, repeat, repeat, repeat.

Saul was led to someone who could get an answer for him.

CHAPTER 9

1 Kings

The Book of Kings continues the history of the time that began in 1ˢᵗ Samuel. King David, as he approached his death, bequeathed the kingdom to his son Solomon. He told Solomon, in 1 Kings, Chapter 2, verse 2, "to be strong, show yourself a man and observe what the Lord your God requires. Walk in his ways, and keep his decrees and commands, his laws, and his requirements, as written in the law of Moses, so that you may prosper in all you do."

Solomon did a good job but felt insecure because of his young age. Still, he struggled to do what he believed God would ask of him. One night, the Lord appeared to Solomon during a dream, and God said, 'Ask for whatever you want me to give you.' Solomon asked for the wisdom he felt he lacked to lead his country. In 1 Kings, Chapter 3, verse 15, "Then Solomon awoke, and he realized it had been a dream." God granted him wisdom and he has become known for it.

Have you ever gone to sleep with a huge problem

that you had no idea the right way to solve? You could do one thing, or you could do another, but which was right? Did you wake in the morning with the answer? This happens a lot. Even, sometimes, if you were not aware you had a problem, but woke with a shift in your path of life clearly in mind and feeling good about it.

We have, in our dream group, a ritual we teach about writing your question for God on a piece of paper, holding it in your hand and praying about it. Tuck it under your pillow and turn out the light; lay your head on your pillow, still praying about it. Go to sleep. Write whatever dreams come to you that night. In the morning, you'll have the answer.

Suppose a friend asks you to dream for him or her. Follow the same procedure. As nature calls, lay still contemplating what had gone through your head just before waking. Write it down as soon as you can. The longer you wait to write, the more of the dream and the answer, you will lose. God and His angels will cloak the answer in a story because it really is not yours to know. The person you are dreaming for will recognize the truth.

God appeared to Solomon in a dream, without being called. God does this with us also. He knows what is bothering us before we do. Some questions He has answered have been as simple as, "Why can't I remember my dreams?" I have found that nothing is too simple for an answer to come to us. If it is important to us, it will be answered. Often there is another way of looking at the problem that you might never have considered had you not asked God, a small bit of the wisdom Solomon received. I found that the mere act of asking will reopen doors between you and God. In my book "God Speaks In Dreams," I've recounted several stories of the question and answer type that were either for me or for another person who had asked for guidance, and also listed the answers we received.

It is important to honor this dream or set of dreams, in some way. Write it down. If there is a food, I'd either add or delete it from my diet. Draw a picture, start a collection of dream symbols and share the dream with a trusted person. Rewards will come.

Rewards, I have found, will show up in life. Rewards come that set you closer to your true path through life because you're finally turning to God. For instance, as I watched my canvas building equipment being driven away down my street. My heart was heavy as I had failed at this endeavor. Within minutes, the mailman arrived and in his hands was an invitation to write for a sporting magazine. This was a career that lasted for several years and gradually morphed into writing books about dreams and also a young adult fiction, plays, and giving lectures about dreams.

As I said before, God leads you step by step. If you are tuned in to hearing His voice in your dreams, you are more likely to have that better life – right here on earth.

Also, in this story of Solomon's dream, God says "Since you have asked for guidance to help your people, and not for long life or wealth for yourself, nor have asked for the death of your enemies but for discernment in administering justice, I will do what you have asked." In addition, God promised to give what Solomon needed, wisdom, not exactly what he asked for. Who knows better than God what we really need? Sometimes I have been surprised by the superiority of what God gave me, compared to what I thought I wanted or needed.

I wish I had read this and understood the verse long before I asked for lottery numbers. With so many wonderful things that were coming into my life, by the grace of God, I asked before falling asleep for the winning lottery numbers. In a dream, I was given numbers and the next day I played those numbers. I lost. Amazed that my God had left me hanging, I asked the next night, "Why did you give me the wrong numbers?" A voice came before my head hit the pillow, "You have to learn to earn your money."

The directions are right there in your dreams.

Our Jungian friend, Katy, would add that there are many gifts within each of our personalities, some have become repressed, now known as our shadow, that wait for us to explore and find them. Some gifts have not yet been discovered on our life journey of emotional and spiritual growth. If we face our fears and challenges, new gifts will arise for us. Our shadow can be very beneficial to us.

A woman had her shadow side appear in the form of a strange man following her. It had been a recurring dream for quite a while. This was told at a talk I was giving on dreams. We all could see clearly that this man was a part of her that was giving her an opportunity to set him free. Perhaps it was a talent she'd denied, an attitude she'd suppressed, or a job that she could easily do that would change her life. Only she would know for sure. She could go back into the dream and ask him what he wanted of her, similar to Jacob's fighting in the wheel of his dream.

This person may have reached an age where a new job was not physically feasible. I feel the simple recognition of opportunities missed can open a dialog with your creator. Life does not end with death. What job will you be doing in Heaven?

CHAPTER 10

Job 4:13

"Amid disquieting dreams in the night, when deep sleep falls on men, fear and trembling seized me and made all my bones shake. A spirit glided past my face, and the hair on my body stood on end. It stopped, but I could not tell what it was. A form stood before my eyes, and I heard a hushed voice."

This came to Job amid all his other problems and questioning of the torments he (a God-fearing man) was suffering. I have had similar dreams or happenings in my life. I've heard other people report the same. If you handle it right, ask God to take them away, it will not happen again. But there may be something worth learning from these spirits.

I had been working steadily with my dreams, God and meditations to get on the path for which I was intended. One night, as I slept, I, too, heard a soft voice. I opened my eyes to see three figures standing at the foot of my bed. Okay, I'm human, and a girl, as if that should make me a member of the weaker sex. I think this apparition would shake anyone to the core. Immediately, I shouted inside myself for God to take this away. They left and have never come back, at least forty-plus years at this date. Had I not been so afraid, could I have learned something from them? I regretted that fear for many years, but, I guess, anyone would have felt the same way. Today, I would ask them questions.

The first point is that if you sincerely work with God, God will work with you. One of the big questions the Bible raises is, why did Job have to suffer so much? First of all, we are not Job. He said he believed, but did he really? It seems to me he was a very negative person. Hopefully, most of us have things we are grateful for and thank God. I was working to get on the path for which God intended me. I do know, from many happenings I've experienced, ask and you'll receive.

For a short while I was also plagued with demons who terrified me when I first went to bed. When my husband joined me, they would disappear. Finally, I got angry. I shouted at God to take them away. I was trying my best to do whatever I perceived my dreams were telling me. God took the spirits away. Still things improved for me.

Has this happened to others? I believe so. I met two who had demons in their dreams in my prison volunteer program. One young lady told how she had been shot in the head as a child and now wears a false eye. All these years, she's hated to go to sleep because ugly beings want to torture her and tear her apart. I told her my story of telling God to take the beings away and how they disappeared forever. That night, she tried this solution. One of her bunk mates said she had witnessed her yelling at God to take them away. They left. Several months later, they were still gone.

Another way to get rid of them comes in a story another inmate and I shared. She told of suffering from nightmares ever since being put in prison, which had been about five years at that point. It came about because of her rape and the death of her husband. She was keeping the whole cell block awake with her screams. My feeling was that five years was long enough to suffer and that she should, hopefully, find some other thing, a moment of joy, to erase these memories and their impact.

The next night that I was teaching a class on dreams, I talked about the movie, "The Wizard of Oz." We would center on the dog, Toto, the Tin Man, Scarecrow, the music and such and just have a good time. Then we would interpret it as if it were a dream. Guess what, she was the only one in the room not familiar with the movie. This could be due to being Spanish? I was stuck. We had a couple of visitors, that night, who called themselves biker-babes. We got to joking over which bike was better, the Harley-Davidson or the Honda. My husband owns a Honda. We did some good-natured joking during my two-hour stay.

The next week, the Spanish lady came in smiling. The guards had awakened her because, for once, she was laughing in her sleep. They wanted to know why. She had been dreaming that she was sitting on a motorbike. In her dreams, she caught the joke and was laughing. My assumption of enough time suffering was right. The biker babes and their motorbikes (the farthest objects ever from her world) broke the cycle.

Our Jungian, Katy, says the Spanish inmate met the "biker babe" energy within and she rode it. She was finally in control, releasing her from the PTSD of rape and death. She could "ride the energy within," and heal. An entirely different outlook freed her spirit.

Maybe the point was about breaking cycles? A knowing of God broke my cycle. Finding joy in the things I was learning about communication with God is what broke my cycle of nasty spirits. Perhaps it did for her also. Perhaps my nasty spirits manifested in all the bad luck things that happened to me from childhood and forward, drove me to my dream work. Some say that everything happens for a reason. I'll have a job delivering dreams from Heaven.

Job goes on. In Chapter 4, verse 20, "between dawn and dusk they (meaning humans) are crushed to pieces: unnoticed they perish forever." Verse 21, "Are not the cords of their tent pulled up, so they die without wisdom?" It is better to get to know God in your dreams before you die. It is our chance to gain some wisdom. The choice is ours. Wisdom comes in dreams if we work to find it.

There is a whole lot more to be said about nightmares. They come to bring you a message from God and once you understand that message, the nightmare never returns, and your life improves. It is too bad Job had to go through what he did and have the negative attitude that he did. At the end of his story, Job did figure it out.

Katy remarks that the story of Job is the story of the human struggle to understand. "Why do bad things happen to good people?" There are actually two endings to the Job story. One is where Job cannot reconcile his challenges for meaning, and second, where Job is blessed again more abundantly. For Katy, it is about full acceptance of the human condition over which we often seem powerless. We are called to give thanks and praise for life itself, always.

CHAPTER 11

Isaiah

Life in the Old Testament talks of war after war, hardship after hardship. One connecting idea is that the men God chooses to bring words of wisdom to various kings and kings to be are the prophets. Isaiah is such a chosen person. He is on earth during the time of David.

In Isaiah 29, verse 7 – 9, it tells something of the properties of dreams. When David's city of Ariel is about to be attacked, Isaiah offers this comfort. "Then the hordes of all the nations that fight against Ariel, that attack her and her fortress and besiege her, will be as it is with a dream, with a vision of the night – as when a hungry man dreams that he is eating, but he awakens, and his hunger remains; as a when a thirsty man dreams that he is drinking but he awakens faint, with his thirst unquenched. So, it will be with the hordes of all the nations that fight against Mt. Zion."

Isaiah goes on to encourage the people to become more spiritual. In other words, although the enemy thinks he can win the war, it is but a dream of his, a wish.

These verses remind me of what we, today, call 'compensation dreams.' God wants us healthy and happy. If we do not have enough of something, like joy, in our lives, He will give it to us in dreams. We awaken, and the joy is gone, but we are left knowing we need joy and a good idea of how to get that joy. That all depends whether we are practicing spirituality, writing and trying to understand our dream messages.

In fact, the next chapter of Isaiah, Chapter 30, it says, "Woe to the obstinate children, declares the Lord, to those who carry out plans that are not mine." You probably wonder how you should know God's plan for you, and I say, write your dreams down and learn how to interpret them!

CHAPTER 12

Daniel

Daniel, in the Bible book carrying his name, was to become a part of King Nebuchadnezzar's court. These were all young, healthy, intelligent Israelites taken from Jerusalem, conquered by the king and were to be trained in the king's religion and culture.

Daniel and three of his friends (all of whom had been renamed) were Belteshazzar, Meshach, Shadrach, and Abednego had resolved not to defile themselves and their God by accepting the king's edict. They rebelled and would have to be accepted for what they were. As a reward, God gave them special knowledge and understanding of all literature and learning, and to Daniel He gave the gift of understanding visions and dreams of all kinds.

We all have dreams; our scientists have proven this. The thing is to spend time learning how to interpret those dreams.

"King Nebuchadnezzar had dreams, his mind was troubled, and he could not sleep," it tells us in Chapter

2, verse 1. When we are troubled, our dreams are more intense. This is because someone much wiser than we are is trying to help us solve our problems. However, you are probably resisting the process. Once you understand the dream and gain the point of view your dreams wish you to change to, the bad dreams go away and your life changes forever for the better.

In verse nine we see that the king not only wants an interpretation of his dream but also wants someone wise enough to recall the dream for him. The privileges of being king! Too bad he did not have the habit of writing down his dreams. He probably could have interpreted them for himself.

This reminds me of Joseph being called out of prison and into the Pharaoh's court to tell the Pharaoh what his dream was and then interpret what it meant.

The king is led to Daniel. Daniel tells the king that only God in Heaven can reveal the mystery of the dream. In other words, a slight rebuke, meaning 'too bad you don't believe in my God.' A spark of God lives within each of us whether we believe it or not. Going back to Daniel's gift, that of being able to recall the king's dream for him and also interpret it, we also can have access to the mystery of others dreams when we learn how to connect with this power within us. The fact that the king believes Daniel can do it, but Daniel has doubts, may only be because Daniel has not done this yet.

In the beginning of my dream work, I was discussing the marvels of my dreams with a friend. This was early in the morning. She asked me to dream for her. I laughed, saying it did not work that way (which sounds similar to

Daniels's reaction). I forgot all about her request, but the Spirit of the dreams did not. That night I had the answer to her question. She worked at Kodak and they were handing out retirement packages to a few employees. That night, as I closed my eyes, I heard a great rumbling noise. My friend came racing around a wall on roller skates with a huge smile on her face and a sign in her hands that read "RETIRED." After telling her what I saw, her husband wanted a dream. My dream work for others rolled on by itself from then on.

For Daniel it meant praying before going to sleep for the king's dream and for the interpretation of the dream. This is also the way I do it, so perhaps that is the lesson for this chapter. The answer came in the night. Daniel was able to describe what the king saw, a statue of many mineral elements, gold, silver, bronze, iron, partially baked clay and iron. A rock from a mountain top, cut out by a hand (not of the earth) rolls down and destroys the statute. In the book of Daniel, it is a long story, summed up somewhat in the Chapter 2, verse 44. "In the time of those kings, the God of Heaven will set up a kingdom that will never be destroyed, nor will it be left to other people. It will crush all those kingdoms (symbolized by the various minerals) and bring them to an end; but the rock will endure forever. This is the meaning of the rock, cut out of a mountain, but not by human hands, a rock that broke the clay/iron, the bronze, the silver and the gold to pieces. Here God has shown the king what will take place in the future. The interpretation is trustworthy." The king was won over to belief, to knowing Daniel's God was the real God, and he changed his ways with regards to which God he worshipped and encouraged his people to do likewise.

If in my dream, I saw a statue made of those same minerals, one thing I might see differently is that the statute is me. The various minerals are different parts of me, of my belief systems. It tickles me that my head would be of gold (my ego self) and my feet are made of clay. When this stone I can't control (God's hand?) smashes it, I could interpret that I am believing wrongly. I'm not doing with my life what God wants me to do, and I can be torn apart by that rock. I would awaken knowing either (1) I do nothing, (2) I let this happen or (3) I begin to make changes. I would either go back to sleep with a prayer for knowledge or sit in meditative silence and wait to have a vision pointing me in either a different direction with my life, or with a different understanding of a situation that is going on in my life. The head being gold might be saying something about my possibly over-valued ego, of which I need to let go, and to spend more time listening to my creator.

You might wonder how I would know the statue is me or you? Everything and everybody in a dream is probably a part of you. You could also be that rock, being rolled into the middle of a bad situation you can change.

I took the dream of the statute made of minerals to my dream group. We came up with other possible interpretations. If the statute dream had been mine, perhaps false idols were being seen. Was I putting my own ego, my golden head, above searching for Gods' answer on the decisions I make, like putting money first, or placing power over something? It might be a prediction of some difficult change coming and I'm being given a chance to emotionally prepare; going up a mountain is a challenge, and could, therefore, be predicting a challenge or recommending a way of facing the challenge. Going up is good. The statute could represent the wealth of the world that can be gone in a minute or something or some attitude in your life that is frozen in time. Be careful what you value. The interpretation that rang strongest with us was that change is coming, knocking down the image we are used to. God is the rock and is bringing the change, and we need to adjust.

Our Jungian, Katy, thinks the rock may be the process of evolution; spiritual, social, and emotional. Jung was a spiritual person. Ultimately evolution controls everything from the beginning of times to the end of times. It is better to accept what we cannot change, and, with courage, we change with evolution's movement. The king is forced to recognize he is a creature, not a ruler over human affairs. Only the God of Evolution, Jesus' Father, has power over changes in human form, living, dying and rising to new life. We are called to do the same spiritually and emotionally. The rock, representing evolution, causes movement and change.

This is told to us once more in the next dream the king had. He dreamed of a beautiful tree that was tall enough to reach Heaven and give refuge to all kinds of people and animals. A spirit came down from Heaven in his dream and told him the tree must be cut down. Daniel reluctantly told the king his reign was ending, he must go live with the animals, and eat grass because his royal authority was going to be taken away from him. In

Chapter 4, verse 33: "He was driven away from people and ate grass like cattle. His body was drenched with the dew of Heaven until his hair grew like the feathers of the eagle and his nails like the claws of a bird."

He lost his sanity until, one day, he praised God for the beauty around him. Then God restored all to him. The king was humbled. The book of Daniel holds many dreams. In the seventh chapter, Daniel recalls one of his own dreams concerning four strange animals that frightened him greatly, and he turned to someone else for an interpretation.

We often do not understand our own dreams. It is like the saying that we are too close to the subject, or that we can't see the forest for the trees. It helps to share your dreams with someone else. They often see something in the dream that we cannot see. In dream groups, as many as ten or twenty explanations for the dream are given. Only the dreamer will know the truth because he or she will get that "ah-ha" feeling like, "why did I not think of that?" God will touch their heart and the dreamer will know the truth of the dream.

Interestingly, this dream of Daniel's may be the first mention of the coming of Jesus. In Chapter 7, verse 13, in the ending of the dream of Daniel's, he tells us, "In my vision at night I looked, and before me was one like a son of man, coming with the clouds of Heaven." Then in verse 14: "He was given authority, glory and sovereign power; all peoples, nations and men of every language worshipped him. His dominion is everlasting and will not pass away and his kingdom will never be destroyed."

In keeping with the theme of this book, if that had

been my dream, or yours, the word 'cloud' jumps out at me. In a cloud you can see nothing. Where in your life are you blinded to something, or by something? In the dream you, a son of God, are coming out of the clouds. Things are becoming clearer for you. Understanding of a situation, or even understanding of your own dreams is finally coming to you and you will have power over your own future. Then again, everything and every person (in the dream) being you, are you the cloud? Are you blocking someone's future, perhaps a son or daughter, because you believe you are the only one with the right answer for their future? In group we mention these things, but, like I said, the dreamer will get that "ah-ha" feeling and know the truth.

Daniel's dreams as told in the Bible are long dreams and include the interpretation. It is well worth reading as the story of Daniel tells of the end of days which is really a change in our lives, not the end of the world. The angel in his vision, in the very last chapter, tells Daniel, "As for you, go your way till the end (when the wars are over) and then at the end of days you will rise to receive your allotted inheritance." In other words, although a lot is said about the end of days; for you and me, life goes on. For me, the afterlife will provide a spot on the committee that gives dreams to people on earth.

CHAPTER 13

Joel 2: verse 28-30

(Repeated word for word in Acts 2: verse 17-18)
These two books both hold the
following words about dreams.
"And afterward, I will pour out my Spirit on all people.
Your sons and daughters will prophesy,
Your old men will dream dreams,
Your young men will see visions.
Even on my servants, both men and women,
I will pour out my Spirit in those days.
I will show wonders in the heavens and on the earth."

There are several places in the Bible where we are warned against dreamers but in no place does it say to not open that dialogue with your creator. Beware of people who try to influence you by their dreams. What is good for one may not be good for another, besides, interpretations can vary from one person's experience to the next. Spend some time and learn to interpret for yourself or in a group of trusted friends.

You might wonder how people interpreted their dreams before dream dictionaries. I wonder when the first one was published. I encourage my groups not to rely on them. They come in handy occasionally but since we all have such different experiences and have reacted to those experiences in different ways, our dream symbols take on a more personal meaning. You might think a universal symbol like a mother might always mean the safety, nurturing, love. But what if your experience of a mother was one of fear, or of being given away? Or perhaps you don't know anything about your mother at all. This is one good example of why people should not take the meanings straight from a dream dictionary. Everyone is different.

Your dreams will help you build your own dream dictionary. Your dreams repeated scenes will reinforce your recognition of messages. For several months I was plagued by snakes in my dreams. Finally, I was able to put that together with my mother-in-law arriving unexpectedly every morning that I had one of those snake dreams. I had my symbol and could laugh, expecting her to drive in the driveway and she did. Symbols do change after a while.

A woman in prison dreamed of flying over a pit with brown and yellow snakes. I gave my only thought, the yellow stood for joy. The women in the room all shouted, "Her name in Joy." She was hanging over a prison of people she regarded as snakes, herself among them. This changed her outlook on life. Read my book "Prison Dreams," for the whole story.

Different meanings come because of different experiences.

CHAPTER 14

Matthew

The Dreams of Matthew are, perhaps the best known of the Christian world. Mary was engaged to Joseph, but had never lain with him, yet she was pregnant. Joseph was debating whether or not to go through with the marriage when he had a dream. In Matthew 1: verses 20 and 21, the story continues. "But after he had considered this, an angel of the Lord appeared to him in a dream and said, "Joseph, son of David, do not be afraid to take Mary home as your wife, because what is conceived in her is from the Holy Spirit. She will give birth to a son, and you are to give him the name Jesus because he will save his people from their sins." Joseph never questioned, but obeyed.

On a note closer to our times, this is confirming the importance of always honoring your dream. Do something about it no matter how small. If the dreams encourage you to do something, perhaps exercise, change your diet, write your memoirs, do the best you can to follow this advice. God would never tell you to do anything that would be harmful to anyone.

I know we are neither Joseph nor Mary, our child being born is not Jesus, but I see another message for us. We have access to our baby before birth. We can also learn about them before they are born. As I anxiously waited for my daughter's second baby to be born, much fear was in the air. It is always harder to watch your daughter prepare to give birth. The date came and went. I put a note under my pillow asking God when it would happen and to let it be easy. I was given a date in my dreams and it came true. We all speak to our babies. We can turn that around, let God or the soul of the baby speak to us.

In Chapter 2: verse 12, the child having been born, He is being honored by the wise men. "And having been warned in a dream not to go back to Herod, they returned to their country by another route." Verse 13 continues with, "When they had gone, an angel of the Lord appeared to Joseph in a dream. "Get up," he said, "take the child and his mother and escape to Egypt. Stay there until I tell you, for Herod is going to search for the child to kill him." Verse 19, says, "After Herod died, an angel of the Lord appeared in a dream to Joseph in Egypt and said. Get up, take the child and his mother and go to the land of Israel for those who are trying to take the child's life are near." Verse 22 also mentions Joseph's dreams and his effort to save the life of the baby.

Your reaction is probably that this is Jesus, so of course God and the angels would protect Him. You've heard this story since childhood. Wouldn't it be wonderful to have God, His angels, the saints and all the heavenly hosts watching out for you like that?

Well you do. We each have someone older, wiser, someone who knows our every deed and thought and still cares about our well-being. These people have been in my dreams, giving me tips to heal, pushing me toward the path God meant for me rather than the one I was on. They helped me to understand the things, situations, people who've hurt me and what to do about it.

Our creator has limitless ability to care for us. There's a reason for the hard-to-understand happenings of life. We learn these reasons through our dreams when we are ready for it, but we need to keep the doors of communication open. This is the way God made us.

There is one more dream in the book of Matthew. In Chapter 27, verse 19 is quite a different kind of dream. This takes place while Pilate is sitting in judgment about which of the men before him to crucify. "While Pilate was sitting on the Judge's seat, his wife sent him this message, don't have anything to do with the innocent man, for I have suffered a great deal today in a dream because of him." Pilate listened to his wife and left the choice up to the crowd.

In order to understand this as a dream lesson for all of us, we must put ourselves in the place of the one who had the dream, Pilate's wife. Our dreams are full of people and things. To understand what Spirit is trying to tell you, you must ask why the neighbor was in your dream when you know so many men and have so many neighbors. The story could have included many alternatives, but this particular neighbor was chosen because; perhaps you need to tell him something, or there is something in his personality that is also in yours.

When I know the person in my dream, I tell them about the dream, even if I need to make a joke out of it. You might be surprised at their reaction. If it is a personality thing, think of their traits, are they impetuous? Perhaps you are about to make a rash decision.

Let's switch the story and suppose Pilate's wife was concerned about the whole situation. Suppose she asked her dreams for a message for her husband about Jesus. It works this way also. You can pray before going to sleep, perhaps write a note to God, put it under your pillow before you go to sleep. Your dreams will often hold an answer. The dream may seem ridiculous but write it down. It will hold meaning for you later.

A circle of friends with whom you can share your dream becomes very important in order to gain perspective regarding the message of the dream. The dream is a revelation of God's truth for us. We want to understand fully the meaning of the dream.

Pilate's wife's dream influenced Pilate's decision-making. It made him fear making the decision on his own. He passed it on. He gave the decision to the angry crowd resulting in the torture and death of an innocent man. Pilate did not want to take responsibility for his own decision. If this was the son of God, Pilate wanted to shield himself. Still he got the death he wanted.

We must listen for the truth of our dreams instead of listening to popular opinion. Ego- based decisions based on power and money are not the way to go, in my opinion.

CHAPTER 15

Acts

Acts 16, verse 9 reads, "During the night Paul had a vision of a man of Macedonia standing and begging him, 'Come to Macedonia and help us." Like I said before, if someone you know is in your dreams, try to talk to this person the next day. Let him know even if you have to present it as a joke. This verse in Acts is taking it further, saying 'help us.'

In Acts 18, verse 9, the Bible says, "One night the Lord spoke to Paul in a vision. Do not be afraid, keep on speaking, do not be silent, for I am with you and no one is going to attack you and harm you because I have many people in this city." God will give you the power to speak the words you know to be true, such as I do in my dream work.

In Acts 22, verse 17, Paul is speaking once more. "When I returned to Jerusalem and was praying at the temple, I fell into a trance and heard the Lord speaking to me. "Quick," He said to me, "leave Jerusalem immediately because they will not accept your testimony about me."

Verse 23 reads, "Go, I will send you far away to the gentiles."

Always give thanks to God whether you understand your dream or not. Try to take steps in the right direction even if it is to simply draw a picture or add to your dream symbol collection. The dream will come back in a different form, perhaps you will better understand it then. You might think the two nights dreams are not connected but keep the window of possibilities open.

Acts is all about the beginning of the Christian Church. Jesus was dead and has risen. Paul and the other disciples travel far and wide to spread the good works Jesus had started. It appears Jesus guided them, sometimes through their dreams.

The purpose of this book is to find the lesson for us, individually, in each of these dreams. In this case, Paul had completely changed his life and was spreading the word of God. It makes sense that some agent of God would help him along the way. If these words are written down to tell you and me something, what can we take away from Paul's experiences?

Would an agent of God, such as an angel or Jesus, guide us along our life's path? These dreams remind me of the step- by-step process our creator uses with me in my own dreams, pushing me to work with my dreams to co-create the life intended for me. While we may think we are getting the whole picture of our own path the first time we see a vision, we actually receive one small piece at a time. Like going to school, we need to know the ABC's before we can put words together.

Reaching my final maturity and experience brings an understanding I hope to share.

When I began my spiritual walk, my dreams had me, a bookkeeper, writing funny stories, incidents in my life. I did it for fun, to see if I could. One day I made a friend, a college president, no less, who would meet me for lunch and edit my work. We met when we coincidently had adjoining booths at a health fair. She taught me the basics of writing. Gradually I was inspired in my dreams to write other things. Since we owned a marina, my words fell to the Great Lakes and the happenings on them. A magazine publisher walked into my life and published my stories and photographs, then a television producer. I thought for sure this was my path. Life went on, things changed, I wrote and directed audience participation plays, tried my hand at young adult fiction; but now dreams are my major focus. One little step at a time, I was led one more step at a time along my path of work for God, and He tells me that I'm not finished yet. There are more things to come, one that includes a mission I may be able to fulfill only after death. So, I also learned that life goes on after death.

I believe this is what the night-time visions of Paul are telling us. Jesus, or God, was leading him step-by-step to an ultimate goal. Paul followed his dreams without question. When you have a dream, honor it by doing something tied in with it. If your dream involves a truck, buy a small toy truck to keep on a shelf of dream symbols. Draw a picture of the dream, you might get a different view of the interpretation. If the dream has a food, either add or take it out of your diet as this may be a health-related dream. If it has a profession you've not considered, try to make room for it as a hobby in your life. You are opening a door. Now wait and see what opportunities God brings to you.

One other aspect of Paul's dreams is the protection given him. It happens for us also. If you are headed down a path that is no good for you, you will get warnings, opportunities to change your mind about things, attitudes are all important. Sometimes the wars of your dreams indicate warring within yourself over which way to go. We get health warnings, by writing your dreams in a journal, you can track how many days between the sight of bugs crawling all over the hood of your car, or your house, and you come down with the flu? I had a certain relative for whom nothing I did was good enough. We argued constantly, and one day, by tracking the dreams written in my journal, I realized I had been warned each time she would show up at my door. From then on, I was ready to deal with her and I actually laughed to myself when she drove in the driveway.

I had a secret between my dreams, the snakes and me. The disagreements did not bother me ever again and neither did the vision of snakes that would foretell she was coming. While we never became great friends (it takes two to change a relationship) I was the last one who sat at her bedside as she passed. You can learn from each person you meet.

CHAPTER 16

Revelations

Some people say that the Book of Revelation is one big dream and must be interpreted symbolically. According to the New International Version (NIV) Study Bible, there are four ways to interpret the Book of Revelation.

The first group they call the Peterists who understand the book exclusively in terms of its First-Century setting, claiming that most of its events have already taken place.

The second group are the Historicists who take it as describing the long chain of events from Patmos to the end of history.

The third group are called the Futurists. They place the book primarily at the end of times.

The fourth is called the Idealists who view it as symbolic pictures of such timeless truths as the victory of good over evil. We are encouraged to read it, for its overall message and resist the temptation to become overly enamored with details.

I evidently read it as a young person, then dismissed

it from my mind because I didn't want to think about the end of times and all those ugly images I didn't understand. As an adult, events in my life brought me a fresh understanding of the book. I came to see one of the stories as a part of my life. You might be touched by another of the stories. Each of our experiences are different and I came to see the book of Revelation as repeating themes in different ways in order to touch us much like our dreams do. If you have a powerful dream that you cannot interpret, it will repeat in a different setting in hopes of getting the message to mean something to you. In time, it will become what we call a 'recurring dream' or even a nightmare.

The story of the locusts came home to me when I was going through a hard time. It seemed I could not please anyone. There was a lot of animosity around me and one day I actually saw locusts in my dream and realized that I could put names to each one of the locusts in the story in Revelation.

That story is about my life and there were lessons to learn. It also gave me a different view of interpreting the other Bible stories than what I had learned in Sunday School.

I found another story in the Book of Judges that also brought home to me that the Bible was talking to me personally on more than one level. I was at a dream conference and the morning speaker read an old poem by a 17th Century man named Hakim. It was titled "The Ten Thousand Idiots Inside Me." It had made an impression on all of us because we were studying Carl Jung's' theories of the committee of souls inside each of us; the inner child, the old crone, the male, the female, the wise old man, and the rest.

After lunch I went to my room, fell asleep and dreamed of the poem. On waking, I picked up the Bible and let it fall open to a chapter of Judges where a land was being taken away from one tribe and possibly given to another. A woman led the fight on one side and God told her to get her ten thousand soldiers to help her defend her position. What hit me was the poem. The story in the Bible was not about yet another war, it was telling those of us who could understand, we have to pull ourselves together and learn to make use of all the various parts buried deep inside us. There are so many similar stories because, like I said, we are all different and what opens me up to truth might not work with you.

My Jungian friend Katy says, "Many call the Bible the Living Word of God. Carol is teaching how this living Word reveals truth to each person through cultures, human experiences, feelings, the thoughts throughout time, two thousand years to the present time and into the future. My dreams and visions are 'My Book of Revelations' between God and my unique self.

CHAPTER 17

The wisdom of Solomon

2 Maccabees and 4 Maccabees
Sirach
From the NRSV Concordance rewritten in 1989

In the Wisdom of Solomon, Chapter 18, verse 17-19, it is written: "At once in nightmares, phantoms appalled them, and un-looked-for fears set upon them and as they flung themselves to the ground, one here, one there, they confessed the reason for their death. For the dreams that tormented them had taught them before they died so that they should not die ignorant of the reason they suffered."

Does this remind you of Job, Chapter 4, verses 20-21, that says, "are not the cords of their tent pulled up, so they die without wisdom"?

There is a bit of wisdom in this passage and that is confessing the reason for their death. I've been doing dream research for many years. People have been made to look at their attitudes and have changed their attitude about things by doing their own dream work. We've learned a lot about ourselves that way and improved our lives. I have concluded that we could be putting St. Peter, who guards the gates of Heaven, out of a job. It was my understanding that we are judged on our lives before we enter the gates and told where to go based on how we've lived our lives. Did we learn what we came here to learn, teach what we came here to teach, prepare ourselves more fully for the life that awaits us beyond the veil called death?

Through dream work, we have been able to judge our own lives properly, and make whatever changes are needed before we die. I envision a bunch of dream workers just sailing right by St. Peter!

This would explain the nightmares. Once we find the message behind the story, make the change in our life, whether it be a change in attitude about something, a change in our vocation, a change in a relationship, a change about how we see ourselves, or whatever it may be, we have gained some wisdom. The nightmares go away and our life changes for the better.

Solomon was indeed wise. So many of us die without ever gaining that wisdom, without knowing why we have suffered.

In a Bible Book called Sirach, the author does not hold my views of dreams. In Chapter 34, verses 1-8, the author has a lot of negative comments to say about people who believe in dreams, even calling us fools. He protects himself though, just in case he is wrong, by saying in verse 6, something about the one exception being if the dream comes from the One Most High. He does leave a door open in case he's wrong. We need to know our creator.

Our Jungian friend Katy says that the author of Sirach was trying to describe the difference between the dreams originating from our personal experience (our unconscious), the collective experience of the world (Jung's theorized collective unconscious), or from the Self (or God) within.

Other of these books are very much filled with dreams. In 2 Esdras, Chapter 14, verses 7 and 8, the author says, "And now I say to you; lay up in your heart the signs that I have shown you, the dreams that you have seen, and the interpretations that you have heard." Do you keep a dream journal? I'll show you how a little later. However, the symbols you collect through your own work may change from time to time but will always stay in your heart.

In the Book of 2 Maccabees, Chapter 15, war is about to break out. Judas Maccabee tried to arm his men with the confidence that only confidence in heavenly help can bring. Verse 11 says, "He armed each of them not so much with confidence in shields and spears as with the inspiration of brave words, and he cheered them all by relating a dream." He reminded them of the times God had helped them before. Does this remind you of the gratitude lists we are suggested to keep?

Verse 16 tells the dream. "In the dream, Jeremiah, the prophet of God, stretched out his right hand and gave to Judas a golden sword, and as he gave it, he addressed him thus; Take this holy sword, a gift from

God, with which you will strike down your adversaries." Judas Maccabees forces went on to win.

We each have access to the golden sword. I feel there comes a time, I'm approaching 80, when it is inevitable that your body will break down and physical struggles will increase.

Earlier in life, between forty-five and fifty, I was diagnosed with a crippling disease, rheumatoid arthritis. I was confined to bed for a time. Then I began my dream study. When I saw a food, I changed my diet. When I could make no sense of constant arguments with a person, I asked God for insight. Was I right? Was I wrong? He gave me a third way of looking at what was really going on. My attitude changed. When I refused to exercise, He showed me a fun way and I gradually grew stronger.

My family had plans that Christmas that did not include us. My husband and I found a small ad for a condo rental on Myrtle Beach. The next few weeks brought me strange dreams. I saw a giraffe, an elephant, planes flying in formation above us, horses in trailers being unloaded next to the beach to be ridden on the beach and I knew I didn't want to walk in their droppings. I also saw a newspaper headline, and most impossible, a friend of mine, named Leroy was playing piano and I said over and over, "That is wonderful, Leroy, Leroy, Leroy."

When we drove into the Myrtle Beach area, there were all the things I'd dreamed about, the giraffe, the elephant, the planes, the horses and a sign welcoming us to Leroy Springs. We picked up a newspaper with the exact same headline. We knew this was meant to be and prepared for the night. That night I had a horrible dream. I sat up most of the night rather than face that dream again. When my husband got up, we discussed the possible meanings. Something had to change but what? The only thing we could think to change was my medicine. We threw the medicine away.

Several weeks later, back at my doctors, the disease was gone from my blood stream. I had been given the golden sword.

If Maccabees dream was my dream, I'd be looking within myself for my golden sword, possibly a talent with which I can win this war of life, or an attitude that needs polishing.

4 Maccabees, 6:5, reads, "A holy man being tortured bore with dignity the beating as a sleeping body who was having a dream." This reminds me of the old phrase, "this too shall pass." If this pain I carry increases, could I face it as if it was a dream? Would I know I could wake up and it might be gone? Then again, spirit knows no physical pain, it cannot be hurt by outside forces. It can sympathize with us. It can help us endure pain. It sometimes tells us how to overcome the pain. I'll have to ask once more and see if, this late in life, it can help me to better live with it. Spirit has warned me, helped me endure and given me ways to stop the pain.

Perhaps the lesson is that our holy spirit cannot be hurt by outside forces, only by things we ourselves do. Also, the problem, whatever it is, health, relationships, finances or whatever else, will pass. Somehow, this elderly holy man in 4 Maccabees knew this too shall pass, one way or another.

As an aside, I recently read a meditation by Emmet Fox about giving parts of a horse to a blind Eskimo and asking him to put it together. He cannot do it without having seen a horse in real life. In other words, it's not over yet, none of us knows the end. Learn from the mistakes we'll make putting it together. Glory in the surprises.

CHAPTER 18

2 Esdras

In 2 Esdras we are told the story of an elderly holy man named Ezra. You might find this chapter interesting as it talks plainly about the end of times (for some people). Ezra's son has fallen dead as he approached the marriage altar. Ezra's grief drove him to the wilderness where he received many visions and predictions. In Chapter 10, verse 59, he is told, "But tomorrow night you shall remain here, and the Most High will show you in dream-visions what the Most High will do to those who inhabit the earth in the last days."

2 Esdras, Chapter 11, verse 1 goes on to describe the dream. "On the second night I had a dream. I saw rising from the sea, an eagle that had twelve feathered wings and three heads..." This goes on to describe what Chapter 10, verse 59, had promised. It is a study in itself and you might find it interesting as it details the 'end of times.' The reading goes on for two more chapters.

Back to the lessons the authors of the various books of the Bible and what they are trying to teach us. This dream in 2 Esdras is all about premonitions. If you keep a journal, go back a few months and read what you wrote. I predict you will find many premonitions of the days since then.

The only book left is Sirach (see Chapter 17) which calls dreamers fools. The author has obviously never had a spiritual experience or a close association with the Trinity despite what that person says. The lesson is that there are doubters everywhere. Like Joseph cautions, be careful who you tell your dreams to.

CHAPTER 19

Afterthoughts

I was walking out of a Bible study with a woman who refused to look at modern, spiritual readings, movies, or essays. Her religion told her they were not Christian; not of the Bible. It came to me that the Bible stopped at a certain place. Why?

The Old Testament is the history of the earth as we know it. The New Testament is the story of the birth of Jesus and organized religion.

In my opinion, the next portion of the Bible, the part about the Holy Spirit that is working in our lives today, is written in many places.

Did God stop talking to us? Did miracles stop taking place? Have there not been what we call historical happenings that shaped the world we live in? Do angels not visit us?

I leave this for you to write. Thank you for listening.

PART TWO

Mechanics

CHAPTER 20

Journaling

1) Chose a journal that will lie flat or fold back on itself. Preferably.

2) On the last two pages make two lists. Title them things you like about yourself, and then, things you do not like about yourself. Over time, you will find these changing.

3) You might start the first page with some inspirational writing or leave room for a table of contents where you will use a key word from your dreams to remind you where to find a dream you've had a while back.

4) On a dream page, write the date and title the dream.

5) Write in the middle of the page leaving wide margins for later notes.

Interpretation

1) Circle all people, places, feelings and colors. Draw a line to the margin and write free association of

your thoughts on these things. What's important is not their role in the dream but rather your general thoughts about each. Examples: a bear is powerful; a snake is slimy and so forth.

2) If it is a person you know, list three personality traits of that person, you may use the actions in the dream to guide you. Dreams use what you know to tell you what you don't know. If the pizza boy is in your dream, what is there about him, why not a neighbor or any other of the many men you know?

3) If it is a house, a kitchen, or other spot, note how you feel about these. Remember the house is you, the car is you (are you driving your own car?) the bus is your traveling community, those you travel through life with. If you are in a train or plane, take this a few steps further. It may be pointing to your vocation or work life.

4) Pick out the oddest thing in the dream, probably the only real message of the dream, and talk with it. Become this thing. Who are you, how do you feel being in this setting, what do you like about being this thing or person, what don't you like, as this object, and finally, what is your biggest wish for yourself as this object?

5) Reread your dream inserting the associations you made rather than the actual noun, feeling, or action.

Remembering your dreams must become a priority in your life. Talk about dreams, read about dreams.

Honor your dreams. If you see or remember nothing but an elephant, draw a picture or find a toy elephant and start a symbol collection.

Dreams will gradually build just like when exercising a muscle, the muscle grows. If no dreams are remembered that first night, do the same the next night. Change the date and write, "I will remember my dreams."

When you have a dream, do not try to understand it then, wait until tomorrow morning. Sometimes during the next day, something may happen that will remind you, "that was my dream."

Many people deny having dreams but everyone dreams. Watch a baby as it sleeps, a puppy, or a kitten. My belief is that this is the way God made us, so we can continue communicating with him after we've come to this earthly plane. My evidence is in the rest of this book.

Sometimes, though, when using this method, we also have access to where we were or what we did before this life. We are all connected much closer than we know. If my daughter is in my dreams, the dream is more likely to be about her than about me. My book, "God Speaks in Dreams, Connect with Him and Each Other," will give you several examples of this.

Sometimes, when my daughter is in my dream it is about my inner child or may be an aspect of myself reflected in my daughter that has been hiding in me. Either way, I should pay attention to it.

Often times, especially as a child, we have been so frightened of our dreams that we've managed to turn them off. Or, perhaps, a simple lack of interest in them has made us forget them. A family who discusses their dreams is a big help to those who participate in understanding real spirituality.

On the other end of the spectrum, perhaps you are being bombarded with dreams and picked up a dream book to see what someone else knew of dreams. This increase in dream activity is often due to stress we are going through in our daily lives. This is the way it worked for me. So, I picked up that first dream book to see what other people knew. The first line of the first book I picked up said that God was speaking to me. I have held this close to my heart ever since and the good that has come proves to me that that statement is true.

CHAPTER 21

Starting a Dream Group

I've mentioned dream groups several times. I find this the best way to understand your dreams. A good size would be between five and fifteen people who meet weekly. It becomes social, educational and intellectual.

Katy says that for her, the group often takes a spiritual direction. We each learn something about God's presence in our own lives.

You need not share the meaning of your dream unless you want to. The person who had the dream is the only one to know the truth of the dream, you'll get that feeling of "ah-ha," why didn't I think of that? Sometimes we are just too close to a subject.

A person with a dream tells the dream. Key words can be written on a board or individuals can keep notes on tablets in their laps. The dream now belongs to the group and each person has a chance to say what the dream would mean if it were "my dream." In fact, it is best to begin your narrative with the words, "If it was my dream…" This way you are neither making judgments on the dreamer, nor are you telling him or her how to live their life. An open mind and acceptance of all possibilities is necessary.

Since we believe God is trying to make our life better and there are the 134 mentions of dreams in the Bible, one would think churches would be leading the path of dream groups but mostly they happen in homes. In the late 1880s to 1920s the Unity Church had a dream section that turned into Silent Unity, a twenty-four-hour prayer service. Charles and Myrtle Fillmore, the founders of Unity believed in going to God (direct to Headquarters) for answers to questions. This was at a time when people were dying like flies from TB. Myrtle, who contracted TB, was able to overcome it.

Dreams were one way they believed in having direct contact with God and getting answers to their problems. Their effort at making dreams part of their church found themselves overwhelmed with requests for dream interpretation.

With the group situation, the group, in each individual church, can be led by themselves and hold the church together on a new, more spiritual level. I earned my degree in Dream Group Leadership from an Episcopal Group. There is a publication named "The Rose" which lists many dream groups across the United States and a few in Europe. Dream groups are regularly held in Episcopal Churches, according to this publication.

There are a very few dream groups being held in prisons and my experience with this situation led to a belief that understanding your dreams was the best, surest way to rehabilitation. In my days of leading such a group, it changed the inmates' perception of their lives and the doors that would open to them. It brought a sense of self-worth. For more information on this you may read my book, "Prison Dreams."

Hopefully the study of dreams will be more common once again, as in the days of the Bible.

CHAPTER 22

Bringing Back Your Dreams

I can't recall being much interested in my dreams growing up. The only talk about dreams was from the grandmother who mostly raised me. Each morning she'd tell me about friends and relatives, long dead, who had visited her during the night and how they'd reminisce about the days when they were growing up. I was very interested in those days. To give you some perspective, Gram had a part-time job playing the piano for the silent movies in the theater in the small Pennsylvania town she lived in. She also spent some time working the switchboard that connected people with their incoming telephone calls and dialed their out-going calls for them.

One night, she and Grandfather both woke to a pounding on the wooden headboard of their bed. The next morning, the telephone operator who had been on duty the night before called to say someone had called at that same hour to say a relative had died. Gram and

Grandfather believed the banging on their headboard was the soul of that person stopping to say goodbye. Still, I never thought of my own dreams. This was hers. Gram took me to church regularly, and later, I made sure my children were raised in a church. I believed.

About mid-life, I found myself with a lot of stress which led to an illness found in my blood. I went into meditation and asked God why. Life had not been so good up to that point and now I was looking forward to living the rest of it as a cripple. Visions took over, three that I could remember, and in them, I was having a good time. I decided to put those visions into my life. I started exercising to music and began my first venture into writing some funny things that happened. I knew the visions were not from my mind. I determined to catch my dreams like Gram had done and see if God had more to tell me.

The key is to make dreams a priority in your life. Talk about them, read books about them, reread the dreams you've had and see if anything new comes to mind. If the dream is a prediction, you won't know it until the event has occurred. Do not be frightened if something bad occurs in your dream. Even the gatherings around the death of someone close needs someone strong to help the others. God does not want us to be sick. Being forewarned eliminates a level of stress. Then, again, death in a dream is seldom physical death but rather a change in someone's life.

If something frightening is shown, it is never as bad as you have seen. You have an opportunity to change things, if you have been on the wrong path. Your attitude can make a huge difference in your reaction, being warned ahead of time, thinking about your possible reactions can change your attitude.

I put a pad and pencil next to my bed, wrote the date and the words, "I will remember my dreams," on the first page. Nothing came through. The next night I did the same. I persisted, often writing just how I felt when I woke; sometimes one or two words were still in my head. Finally, the dreams I could remember came. The first had me going across the Canadian border. The police stopped me and proceeded to search my car. They found illegal hams in my trunk. I got up, wrote it down and went back to sleep. The next morning, reading the dream, I had a good laugh. I was too heavy and did need to get the fat out of my trunk.

The dreams continued and with each I tried to make a change in my life according to what the dream said, or what I thought it said. Sometimes it was about what I thought about myself, what I thought others thought about me, what talents I had or did not have, what food I needed to add or take away from my body. Then opportunities walked in my door, so to speak. An opportunity came to write for money and it changed my life drastically. I was happy, and within two years, the disease was gone from my blood.

The key, after so many years of ignoring my dreams, I see now is persistence. Like any muscle that has been let go, we need to exercise this dream muscle and make it stronger. You can do it also. God is waiting to communicate with you.

CHAPTER 23

Interpretation

No instance in your life is too small for God to take an interest. If it bothers you, it bothers Him. It has been said that someone older and wiser than us, someone who knows all about us and loves us anyway, wants the best for us, health, finances, career and joy. This someone (I call God) speaks to us in dreams and meditation trying to change the way we think about a subject. I often had instances when a subject came up in my dreams that I didn't know bothered me. God knew, and the outcome was rewarding.

Sometimes the scene in the dream is straight forward, perhaps warning us of something to come. I often get predictions of things from half way around the globe. I believe this happens to keep me interested in the dreams. It was neat, at least to my way of thinking, to have advance knowledge of something even though there was nothing I could do about it.

The majority of dreams, however, need interpreting. If I was to tell you to pick up something, for instance, you could easily ignore me. If the scene you see is of that same thing containing a dangerous problem for you, you would find a way to get it removed. It's emotions that move us to make changes.

Another suggestion I strongly make is to study Carl Jung. You will learn to discern your male and female energies, or sides, your shadow (which can be good or bad) and other energies within you, like the crone, the wise man, the mother or father energy, the child, and how God may be using them to tell you something.

Another way to interpret a dream is to become an image in the dream. This was taught to me by Dr. Robert Hoss, another dream researcher and past president of the Association of the Study of Dreams (IASD). Ask yourself questions. Become the image. After each image, I'll give you a few common interpretations from other dream symbol books and then show you what can happen when you become the image.

Bones: Do you have a bone to pick with someone? It can mean strength and your ability to carry your load; bare bones = just give the facts. If you go the route of asking yourself questions as if you are those bones, it might go like this. First describe yourself. If you have ever seen a skeleton, you know what I am. A skeleton's purpose is to hold the flesh and organs of a living body together, but as yet, I don't have a body or through my actions I have lost who I am supposed to be. What I like about myself is that I have the potential to be a body or to be a teaching tool. What my biggest fear is that I'll be forgotten. My biggest wish is that I can find out what my purpose is and fulfill that purpose, be useful. See the comments in "Box" below.

Box: Can mean a boxed or closed-in feeling, unfortunately you are living in the limits of your surroundings, boundaries, a block to your progress; or it can symbolize a gift. Everything in the dream being you, I once heard a dream in a prison class where the dreamer had dreamed of walking through the woods and finding a box that had the bare bones of a person spilling out. Her first instinct was to fold the bones back into the box and hide the box. End of dream. That box and those bones was the situation she had gotten herself into. She is trapped in a box of a cell. Her worth may be that of a bunch of old bones. The woods represented all the issues in her life. Now, in the box of a cell, she could straighten herself out, pack the old dead self away and start working on a new self.

Chicken legs: Legs denote the ability to stand up for one's own rights. Being chicken legs, and if the dream was mine, I would look to where in my life I lack that ability. The dreamer sent the dream to dream circle. In the dream she was to insert raw chicken legs into plastic bags. Someone told her that she was doing it wrong. We tried to find meaning within the dream circle, but this had us stumped. We asked ourselves questions like, 'were her legs strong enough to carry her body?' She seemed to have no problem in that area. We let the dream go and a week later found her with a bad cold or flu. One of the dream group members, living close by, fed her chicken soup and other beverages. She recovered, and we decided the dream was a warning this was in her future.

Cookie: Even the most normal dream, that of the past, will hold something unusual. This dream had me eating cookies. I tried talking to the cookie as if I was the cookie. I described myself as round and chocolate chip. My purpose in life, so I told myself, was to be eaten. What I did not like about being a cookie was the short life I would have. What I liked about being a chocolate chip cookie was the joy I was able to bring to others. My biggest fear was being dropped on the floor and crushed under someone's feet. Hmmm. Was there somewhere in my life where this was a real fear? The greatest joy I had as a cookie was wishing I could last forever and bring more people joy. My answer to the dream was to step out of my circle and see where I might help someone else with their dreams.

Doors: Doors in a dream are an invitation to something new. Go back into the dream and open that door. You have a new opportunity to bring something better into your life, make room for something you have always wanted to do. Watch your life for a chance at something that will increase your good health, your joy, or in some other way you never expected. In a dream, a person is walking through a house and comes to a closed door. If I take the part of the door, I first describe myself. I'm a plain door inside a house. My purpose is to lead someone into another space, a space they have never been. What I like about being a door is that I can swing open or shut, I offer a different view of things. What I don't like, in this dream, the person is not making use of me. My biggest wish is that he or she would open me and see the space in their life that they can fill any way they want. Or they find antiques worth a lot of money and it would solve their financial problems.

Egg: The common interpretation for an egg is new growth or opportunity. Talking to the dreamer as the egg can open other doors of understanding. Another lady, not in prison, dreamed of holding an egg with a piece of shell missing. The people around her spoke of throwing it away, frying it; of using it anyway. She thought of herself as the egg, like thousands of other eggs only with that one tender, vulnerable spot. Everyone was telling her what to do. If she could do anything she wanted, she would hatch into a real bird and fly away. This held great meaning for her life.

Frog: Can be an ancient symbol of something unclean in your life, or your prince that needs kissing is about to make an entrance in your life. It can be a play on words such as being a little frog in a big pond. One of the most common ways to decipher your dream, after writing it, is to imagine yourself as every person and everything contained in the dream. I once heard a dream where a lady walked into a child's bedroom that had wall paper full of frogs. There was a toy frog on the floor. As she thought of herself as the toy frog, she was glad she was not like the rubber-stamped ones on the paper and that she could move around and be held by the child. If she was the child, she'd be glad when she and the frog became grown up, bringing freedom, clearer thinking, less of the sameness of that room, more of the ability to leave the room. It meant a lot to her to think she could think for herself and not be a copy of someone else – or sit on the walls like someone else expected of her.

Gold: There was a lot of the color gold in my dream and my mind went to the metal, gold. Gold must be mined and, to me, something good is being formed, dug out of my unconscious. Good days are ahead.

Gutter: A common meaning applied to the vision of a gutter is the saying about being stuck in a bad place. To describe myself, I am a half pipe that goes around a house just below the roof. My purpose in life is to catch the rain and funnel it to the corners of the house. What I don't like about being a gutter is that often I am forgotten, not kept clean of leaves and other trash. My biggest fear, if I was the gutter, is the freezing icicles that can drag me down in the winter. My biggest wish is that I could add to the beauty of the house and be attended to faithfully and that people would appreciate the job that I do. In all, if you had this dream, is there some area of your life where you would like more appreciation for what you do?

Dead leaves: Old issues may be dead but are not forgotten. Sweep them away. The dream that prompted this addition was that I was going swimming in the pool and found the bottom of the pool thick with dirty, dead leaves. To describe myself, I'd first have to say I was a useless old leaf, or perhaps there was an issue in my life that was dirtying my life. This must be cleaned up in order to continue my activities in a pleasant manner. My purpose, as an old leaf is to keep alive old memories of things best cleaned up and forgotten. What I don't like about being a dead leaf is that I take up room in the pool of this small life that could be free of old issues and memories. Someone could clean me up and have a more fun-filled, healthy, and successful life. What I like about these old leaves is the ability to re-live the past and perhaps learn something from them. My biggest fear, though, is in the remembering, keeping these issues alive. It is best to defeat them, not let them become a pattern in my life. My biggest wish is to have a clean pool, a clean emotional and spiritual place to rest my heart.

Lizard: perhaps something to fear; the little lizards in Florida are a delight to most; if a child catches them by the tail, the tail will release from its body and grow back. Perhaps we have something we need to let go. I once dreamed of watching a small lizard climbing up the inside of a window pane in my kitchen. First, I described myself as the lizard which was small compared to the big world outside that window. I liked that I could climb up (up is good) and maneuver to see more and more. That is life as our maturity grows. What I did not like was being trapped inside. Where in my life did I feel trapped? My biggest fear was falling. If I could have anything in the world, as that lizard, it was to be outside, free and enjoying Gods' world more than I was. In fact, the dream ended with a man gently taking the lizard outside and letting it loose. The man, my masculine side, would show me how to solve my problems. One of my wishes will soon come true.

Then I did the same with the other images and people in that dream. It gave me a much clearer view of who I really was and what I needed from life.

A man: If a man you know is in your dream, you must ask why him; why not one of the many other men you know? Look at his personality. Your clue may lie there. If he is shy, silent, industrious, look to those traits in yourself. Then look at his place in the dream. Are his actions in the dream something you should think about for your own life?

Person (see man); If someone you know is in your dream, you might contact this person and tell him the dream. It may be a message for that person instead of for you.

Rock: Common interpretations include being changeless, solid, unbending, a barrier, or a difficulty. A woman in my dream group dreamed of walking a path between high mountains, going up (that's important) when she sees a rock that is shiny, flat on one side like a grave marker but with no writing. We decided on the stone as the odd object in the dream and she became the rock. She said, "I'm sitting by the side of the road." (Did she feel this way in waking life, a watcher rather than a participant?) "I can see lots of feet moving around me and a river flowing by with boats of people going somewhere. One side of me is polished marble or granite with beautiful designs. The other side of me is just a natural rock. As for a purpose, I seem to be a marker although there are no words on me. I don't like not being aware of my purpose in life. I like that I am solid and strong. My biggest fear is that nobody will stop to see me. My greatest wish is that they see that although I am just a rough stone on one side, they will realize my inner beauty and realize they also have inner beauty." This is the message I'd like to bring to everyone.

Vehicles: A car can be your very personal ride through life. One important question is whether you are in the driver's seat. A bus may be pointing out your place in your community, or your job, your friends or your family. In my own dreams I was once in the back seat of a convertible, my son and his girlfriend whom I loved were in the front. So, it was about their life, not mine. The car was going backward over a cliff. In order to interpret it, I became the car, I'm not in control. The relationship is going backwards and may die at the bottom of the cliff. My wishes did not matter in this instance. In life, the relationship did end.

Along the same line, a woman in my dream group dreamed of taking a trip on a hay wagon. She'd never been on one. So, we asked her to try to think like this hay wagon in her dream. She described herself as a flat wagon pulled by a tractor. Her purpose was after the harvest of hay or straw, she'd be loaded for the care and feeding of farm animals. She says she'd be rolled out and bales of hay would be loaded on her. What she liked about being the hay wagon was that she was the most important piece on the farm. There was not a farm without one. What she did not like was sitting in a corner alone most of the time. Her biggest fear was that they'd never need her. Her biggest wish was to be more useful. She could see a lot of her life as she was living it in these statements and ideas came to get her biggest wish.

War: A common interpretation might be a need to forgive yourself for something. If a war is raging around you in your dreams, ask what kind of a war is going on in your home life, your work life, or maybe you are trying to decide something? An attitude may be causing you trouble even though you don't see it that way.

Dream dictionaries are sometimes helpful but can also be a hindrance. They may stop you from thinking of other reasons for a symbol to be in your dream. Use them as a last resort, to jog your thoughts when nothing else is coming.

ABOUT THE AUTHOR

Carol Oschmann, the author of the book, is joined by remarks made by Jungian and an ex-communicated Roman Catholic Woman Priest, Katy Zatsick.

Carol became interested in Dreams in 1985 when a spiritual experience convinced her to find out what others knew about dreams. This story is told in her first book, *God Speaks in Dreams: Connect with Him And Each Other.* She received a physical healing, financial healing, changed the way she viewed herself and others and changed the path of her life. She has since attended Haden Institute where she received a degree in Dream Group Leadership; she's given many lectures on dreams; taught classes at the local community college on dreams; led several weekly dream groups; written a second book, *Prison Dreams,* which told of her years spent volunteering at a women's prison teaching the inmates to find self-worth by learning to properly interpret their dreams. This book, *Prison Dreams,* won First Place in 2010 Contest from the National League of American Pen Women. Carol can be reached at oschmann@verizon.net.

Mentioned often in this book is Katy Zatsick, a Roman Catholic Woman Priest, who has had a life-long interest in dreams. She has studied the work of Carl Jung and is a member of the Carl Jung Society of Sarasota, Florida, besides being a participant in Carol's current weekly dream circle. Katy was a patient in psychoanalysis for ten years with Dr. Suswik. The work in therapy centered on dreams and their interpretation. She lives in Sun City Center, Florida, and, as a Roman Catholic Woman Priest, she uses dreams in spiritual direction. Katy can be reached at katyrcwp@tampabay.rr.com.

Made in the USA
Coppell, TX
01 July 2023

18646820R00074